Shakespeare's
Rhetoric of
Comic Character

Shakespeare's Rhetoric of Comic Character

Dramatic convention in
Classical and Renaissance comedy

Karen Newman

Methuen   New York and London

First published in 1985 by
Methuen Inc.
733 Third Avenue, New York
NY 10017

Published in Great Britain by
Methuen & Co.
11 New Fetter Lane,
London EC4P 4EE

Typeset by Activity Ltd, Salisbury, Wilts.
Printed in Great Britain
at the University Press, Cambridge

Library of Congress Cataloging in Publication Data

Newman, Karen, 1949–
Shakespeare's rhetoric of comic character.
Bibliography: p.
Includes index.
1. Shakespeare, William, 1564–1616—Comedies.
2. Comedy.   I. Title.
PR2981.N48   1985   822.3'3   84-27183

ISBN 0-416-37990-7

British Library Cataloguing in Publication Data

Newman, Karen
Shakespeare's rhetoric of comic character:
dramatic convention in classical and
renaissance comedy.
1. Shakespeare, William—Comedies
I. Title
822.3'3   PR2981

ISBN 0-416-37990-7

for Tom

Contents

	Acknowledgments	viii
	A note on texts	x
	Introduction	1
1	The inward springs:	
	Measure for Measure II, ii, 162–87	7
2	Comic plot conventions in *Measure for Measure*	20
3	Menander and New Comedy	30
4	Plautus and Terence	42
5	The enchantments of Circe	57
6	'And all their minds transfigur'd':	
	Shakespeare's early comedies	77
7	Magic versus time:	
	As You Like It and *Twelfth Night*	94
8	Mistaking in *Much Ado*	109
9	Shakespeare's rhetoric of consciousness	121
	Notes	129
	Index of plays discussed	149
	General index	151

Acknowledgments

It is my pleasure to acknowledge the many debts and obligations this book owes to others. Thanks are due to Harvard University for the Mellon Faculty Fellowship (1980–1), and to Brown University for the Henry Merritt Wriston grant (Fall, 1981), which allowed me the leisure to refine my argument and most importantly, to write. My general dependence on past scholarship is indicated in the notes to my text, but more personal debts require acknowledgment separately. I have gathered untold benefits from Jonas Barish, whose example as both scholar and teacher first encouraged this study of Shakespeare. His reading of my manuscript at various stages has been invaluable both for its patience with my early confusions and its faith in the ultimate text. I am also grateful to Louise George Clubb who first introduced me to the richness of Italian Renaissance comedy and its relationships with Elizabethan drama; to W. S. Anderson, whose early course on Virgil prompted me to pursue the classics; to Barbara Lewalski and Walter Cohen who read my manuscript and made many attentive suggestions; to my colleagues at Brown who have provided enthusiastic intellectual support and good fellowship. Special thanks go to Steve Goodwin for his meticulous translations from the Greek, and to E. Walter Hopton for his conscientious service in the final stages of preparing the typescript. I also owe a more general debt to Françoise Cusin Jankowski, an early teacher and present friend.

And there are other kinds of debts: to my friends, Carol Cook and Betsy Fox Zimmerman, and to my husband, Thomas R. Brooks.

A note on texts

I have used the Arden editions of Shakespeare's texts (London, Methuen); quotations from Menander, Plautus and Terence are from the Oxford Classical Texts, but typeface has been standardized. In addition, I have used the following editions and translations:

Donatus, *Commentum Terenti*, Lipsiae, 1905.
La Commedia degl'Ingannati, ed. Florindo Cerreta, Firenze, 1980.
Bargagli Girolamo, *La Pellegrina*, ed. Florindo Cerreta, Firenze, 1971.
Clyomon and Clamydes, ed. Betty J. Littleton, The Hague, 1968.
The Rope and Other Plays, trans. E. F. Watling, New York, 1964, rpt. 1977.
The Pot of Gold and Other Plays, trans. E. F. Watling, New York, 1977.
The Comedies of Terence, trans. Frank O. Copley, Indianapolis, IN, 1976.
Five Italian Renaissance Comedies, ed. and trans. Bruce Penman, New York, 1978.

Introduction

At least since Samuel Johnson commended Shakespeare's characters for their naturalness and criticized his plots for their conventionality,[1] audiences have remarked what seems a fundamental contradiction in Shakespeare's comedy between character and convention. Why, we ask, in the midst of the wonderful coincidences and arbitrary improbabilities of plot, the inherited paradigms of classical and Italian comedy, do we leave the theatre or study assured that Shakespeare's characters develop and change? And perhaps more importantly, is their development really antithetical to the conventions and devices of comic drama?

Character is required in drama because action requires agents. Contemporary theoretical work on character, though primarily directed at narrative, has seized upon this Aristotelean observation to repudiate the notion of character as an individual who changes or develops, with an inner life or psychology. Critics have explained character as agency or function subordinate to action and have devalued *vraisemblance* and representation in characterization. Influenced by

Propp's work on the Russian folktale and Lévi-Strauss's anthropology, which views the self 'more and more as a construct, the result of systems of convention',[2] they have emphasized characters not as beings, but as agents determined by their relation to particular actions. The linguistic categories of syntax and paradigm are superimposed on a text or group of texts, and characters are defined in relation to this overall structure. So, for example, Todorov describes characters in terms of 'predications'; Greimas, writing on medieval romance, calls them *actants* which participate in paradigmatic and syntagmatic relations.[3] To show an interest in a complex character reveals a failure of critical nerve, an irresistible and sentimental urge to give in to the seductive power of mimesis. But, as Roland Barthes points out in an essay reviewing contemporary theories of character, a character who is both subject and object, a self seeking his own identity, resists structural analysis of the kind practiced by Todorov and Greimas. Shakespeare's plays are peopled with just such characters.[4]

Even a cursory look at the history of Shakespearean criticism, from Dryden and Johnson, to Schlegel and Bradley, to recent psychoanalytic approaches, suggests that readers perceive his characters as lifelike. The persistence of such judgments, from the seventeenth century to the present day, suggests that we cannot simply dismiss them as culturally determined by a particular period or even ideology which values the 'realistic'. Our sense of dramatic character is shaped by many features of a text and its performance: dialogue; interaction among characters; the alternation of scenes; and the way in which actions are performed, from their context and the explanations surrounding them, to the gestures and other elements of spectacle which mold our understanding. But Shakespeare's characters are marked by what we might call a residue beyond their function (Lt. *fungor*, to perform) as agents, beyond their relations to specific actions. This residue or excess – for what we perceive can be conceived metaphorically as both greater than the action or plot, and as what is left over, what continues in our experience after the action is complete – I would argue, is what audiences have called the lifelikeness of Shakespearean character.

In *The Compleat Gentleman* (1622), Henry Peacham claimed that a man is his mind, and readers of Shakespeare have long recognized the important role our sense of a character's inner life plays in creating the lifelike. Though many features of language contribute to characterization[5] – dialect or jargon, meter, the use of a repeated figure or image, allusion, the places or *topoi* of decorum[6] – perhaps the most common strategy Shakespeare uses to create the illusion of mental life and complex character is the soliloquy. Critics say casually that a soliloquy presents the thoughts of a given character, but they have seldom looked carefully at the rhetorical features which represent an inner life to both reader and audience. Wolfgang Clemen has analyzed the features and role of tragic soliloquies in the larger dramatic structure of pre-Shakespearean and early Shakespearean tragedy,[7] but soliloquies in the comedies have not received the attention they deserve. Set speech master-pieces such as Launce's to his dog, or Costard's satiric lament on his remuneration in *Love's Labour's Lost*, have received considerable individual attention, but have limited usefulness for the purposes of this study.[8] The features which distinguish these monologues – the word play, quibbles, dialect or jargon, repeated rhetorical figures – make them vivid, but these characters rarely have a significant function in their comic plots; they are objects, not processes.[9] I analyze and compare protagonists' soliloquies in the comedies to discern shared rhetorical features and to discover their position and function in conventional comic plots.

By focusing on protagonists' soliloquies, perhaps we risk taking a skewed perspective of Shakespeare's comic practice. We miss, for example, the experience we have of Rosalind as a complex character because Shakespeare uses strategies other than the soliloquy or monologue to create Rosalind's mental life; we miss Falstaff because his comic soliloquies are part of a different genre, the history play; and we miss such colorful characters as Juliet's Nurse or Parolles in *All's Well*. But by limiting our study to the soliloquies and monologues of comic protagonists and their intersection with the conventional comic plot, we stand to land a prize whose features and anatomy we can examine intimately to see details of structure, color and shape we might otherwise miss if we threw our net wider and hoped for a bigger catch.

In his study of pre-Shakespearean soliloquy, Clemen observes the importance of set speeches for presenting characters, their states of mind and motives of action. He defines a set speech as 'any continuous spoken passage that stands out noticeably from the general run of the dialogue by reason of its length and structure, its theme or its significance'.[10] Such a definition would include not only soliloquies, but certain asides and what we might term more generally monologic dialogue, fragments of dialogue in which a character speaks apparently to himself rather than to his interlocutor.[11] Soliloquies and monologic fragments, characteristic of what Clemen terms rhetorical rather than realistic drama, nevertheless individualize Shakespeare's characters and endow them with motive and intention, conflict and complexity. In other words, they communicate a mental life which we perceive as lifelike far more effectively than simple description of a psychic event. To communicate the sense of a character's inner life requires a different mode of presentation. Paradoxically these dramatic speeches, though outside the dialogue structure of the play, possess linguistic features which class them with dialogue – in other words, they present a mind in conflict with itself by thematizing the theatrical conventions of dialogue.[12] Practitioners and theoreticians of the narrative interior monologue long ago recognized that the illusion of mental activity is best conveyed by dialogue.[13]

Particular pragmatic, grammatical and rhetorical features classify an utterance as dialogue. Linguists note as most important pronominal contrasts of 'I' and 'you', questions, temporal markers and verb tenses which indicate the relation of the utterance to its context, and an unhomogeneous structure in which the syntactic and semantic patterns of assertion and response alternate to suggest the presence of two minds or points of view. This final aspect of dialogue, sometimes called semantic reversal, is also its most varied and complex.[14] In addition to the features of dialogue, Shakespearean soliloquies and monologic fragments also often manifest a preponderance of expressive elements of language which communicate intense emotion. By analyzing such speeches, we can construct a typology or rhetoric of Shakespearean character in the comedies.[15] But however important such rhetorical strategies of dialogue and inner debate may be when independently considered, to understand their larger effect in creating lifelike characters we must examine these materials within the coherent structure and shape of a given plot.

The rhetorical features of soliloquy and its place in conventional comic plots have a long history, and part of my purpose in this study has been to place Shakespeare's comic practice in a larger historical frame. In his excellent book, *Shakespeare and the Traditions of Comedy*, L. G. Salingar claims that Shakespeare's characters, unlike those of classical and Italian comedy, possess the 'quality of an inner life'.[16] But the rhetoric of inner life which characterizes the comic soliloquy was not new to Shakespeare; it is part of a long tradition, inherited from ancient comic practice and exploited by Italian Renaissance comic dramatists. I begin, therefore, by identifying the features of Shakespeare's rhetoric of inner debate in comic soliloquy in *Measure for Measure* because its critical history provides perhaps the best example of the conflict between character and convention which has dogged criticism of the comedies. Even today commentators persist in rebuking Shakespeare for abandoning realistic characterization in order to bring about a conventional happy ending in this play.[17] I go on to place this rhetoric of comic character within the context of literary history by examining representative classical and Italian comedies and the received opinions about New Comic characterization in the commentaries. Finally I return to Shakespeare's plays to demonstrate how he used inherited comic conventions, not in opposition to realistic characterization, but as a strategy for accomplishing it. Instead of a contradiction between conventional plotting and realistic characterization, the conflict Johnson and others have so often observed in Shakespeare's comedy is between two different and opposing conventions, one which foregrounds itself and its artifice, the other which conceals itself by seeming 'real'.

Instead of simply asserting the value of representation, as have generations of Shakespeareans, or repudiating it, as have contemporary theoreticians, I attempt to describe the conventional features of comic characterization which represent a character's inner life.[18] Paradoxically, we discover, a character often becomes more real by doing what are patently unrealistic things – speaking soliloquies, thinking aloud, and the like. My aim is to demonstrate the artifice Shakespeare uses to convey thought and feeling, for like E. H. Gombrich,

> I believe that we are in real danger of losing contact with the great masters of the past if we accept the fashionable doctrine that such matters never had anything to do with art. The very reason why the representation of nature can now be looked upon as something commonplace should be of the greatest interest to the historian.[19]

Just as the visual image has become cheap, so the verbal conventions of the real have lost their value. But the critical intuitions about Shakespeare's realistic characters must not be simply dismissed as naive. Dramatists and novelists alike have long labored to create the illusion of the lifelike and natural; critics and readers have too often accepted that illusion as real because Shakespeare was a master of illusion.

1

The inward springs: *Measure for Measure* II, ii, 162–87

Goethe has ingeniously compared Shakespeare's characters to watches with crystalline plates and cases which, while they point out the hours as correctly as other watches, enable us at the same time to perceive the inward springs whereby all this is accomplished.

(Schlegel, *Lectures on Dramatic Art and Literature*)

Goethe's comparison suggests that Shakespeare dramatizes the dynamics of the inner life; he portrays a character's inner self as process. Auden remarks that 'the difference between Shakespeare's tragedies and comedies is not that the characters suffer in the one and not in the other, but that in comedy the suffering leads to self-knowledge, repentance, forgiveness, love, and in tragedy it leads in the opposite direction into self-blindness, defiance, hatred'.[1] It is the process of those changes in his comic protagonists which we will be analyzing, using *Measure for Measure* as our example.

Consider the following soliloquy from *Measure for Measure* which dramatizes Angelo's recognition of his desire for the novice Isabella:[2]

> From thee: even from thy virtue!
> What's this? What's this? Is this her fault, or mine?
> The tempter, or the tempted, who sins most, ha?
> Not she; nor doth she tempt; but it is I   165
> That, lying by the violet in the sun,
> Do as the carrion does, not as the flower,
> Corrupt with virtuous season. Can it be
> That modesty may more betray our sense
> Than woman's lightness? Having waste ground enough,   170
> Shall we desire to raze the sanctuary
> And pitch our evils there? O fie, fie, fie!
> What dost thou? or what art thou, Angelo?
> Dost thou desire her foully for those things
> That make her good? O, let her brother live!   175
> Thieves for their robbery have authority,
> When judges steal themselves. What, do I love her,
> That I desire to hear her speak again?
> And feast upon her eyes? What is't I dream on? /
> O cunning enemy, that, to catch a saint,   180
> With saints dost bait thy hook! Most dangerous
> Is that temptation that doth goad us on
> To sin in loving virtue. Never could the strumpet
> With all her double vigour, art and nature,
> Once stir my temper: but this virtuous maid   185
> Subdues me quite. Ever till now
> When men were fond, I smil'd and wonder'd how.[3]
>
> (II, ii, 162–87)

The opposition between speaker and hearer or 'I' and 'you', the most common feature of dialogue, is manifest in this soliloquy in the semantic pattern characteristic of self-address. Angelo begins by using the first person, but in lines 173–5, he shifts to the second person pronoun 'thou' and poses himself a series of questions. This alternation between the first and second person pronouns in reference to the same antecedent, here Angelo, characterizes soliloquies which attempt to represent mental life. Interrogatives abound in this speech, but they are exclamatory, not performative; rather than requests for information, they are rhetorical questions which communicate a sense of urgency and emotional tension. But as questions they also posit a speaker and hearer. Angelo himself assumes both roles in a dialogue of the mind in which his chiding interrogation of self suggests the gnomic utterances of conscience or authority.

If we look carefully at the series of rhetorical questions which begins in line 168, we find that the first person 'I' has become plural. To whom, we ask, does 'our' in line 169 refer? Characteristically in Shakespeare the first person plural used by the head of state is a royal 'we', the 'we' of public acts and proclamations. But Angelo is certainly not talking here about public business, nor does he use any but a genuine 'we' in the scenes preceding this speech (I, i, 61, 82; II, i, 17). The question at lines 168–70 seems to exclude women from the group to which 'our' and later 'we' refer. The first person plural apparently constitutes a generic statement or utterance about men in general, of whom Angelo is one. We are still witnessing a dialogue with self, but self as part of a larger category: men who feel desire and seek sexual gratification – for Angelo at least, men in general. The speech represents both Angelo in self-address and Angelo creating an audience larger than himself, an audience of common men.[4] This movement from the personal to the social has powerful effect, for it unites Angelo for the first time in the play with common humanity. Shakespeare has been at pains earlier to show us that Angelo considers himself anomalous; this locution testifies to his discovery of his humanity. And it is one of the often noted ironies of the play that this discovery leads him to make his foul proposition to Isabella.

The first person plural also implies a reader complicit with such universalizing rhetoric. As audience we are led by these pronouns, and by the strictly generic statement later in the speech, 'Thieves for their robbery have authority,/When judges steal themselves', to accept the moral judgments which

Angelo makes and the ethical standard which he here represents. The effect of these rhetorical questions and the first person plural pronouns is to communicate Angelo's feelings and to generate sympathy in the audience by setting those feelings in a larger context of masculine temptation and human frailty.[5]

The most emphatic instance of self-address falls in the exact center of the soliloquy: 'What dost thou? or what art thou, Angelo?' The repeated questions posed to the self, with only a change in the verb, emphasize the meaning of the line. In the first half, Angelo asks himself simply what he is doing. He questions his own actions and feelings. The shift to the copula turns the question into an existential one, for in the second half-line Angelo questions not simply his behavior, but his very being. The juxtaposition of the two interrogatives suggests the struggle in his mind between man as rational agent and man as instinctual beast. The exclamatory 'O' and subjunctive with imperative force which follow in line 175 emphasize the I/you opposition, for Angelo is beseeching himself on Claudio's behalf. Here where the grammar most emphatically resembles dialogue, its semantics are most like the interior monologue in attempting to enact psychic process.[6]

Angelo's soliloquy also manifests other features of dialogue. Demonstrative pronouns, temporal markers and verb tenses connect this speech to its context, the preceding interview with Isabella in which she asks mercy for her brother Claudio. The very first lines presuppose Isabella's preceding words, 'Save your honour', for in order to understand Angelo's 'From thee: even from thy virtue!' we must remember Isabella's words of valediction. In line 163, the repeated pronoun 'this' refers emphatically to the previous scene, to Angelo's 'breeding sense' and his continuing response to Isabella after her departure. As audience or reader, we must supply the antecedent, and in doing so, we situate the speech in its larger context in the play. We also find such orienting locutions later in the contrasted past and present of 'never ... once' and 'ever ... til now'. These elements serve to locate the soliloquy in time and with reference to the specific situation of Angelo's past reputation as an ascetic and his newly discovered passion for Isabella.

The third aspect of dialogue is also its most complex. Semantic reversals occur on the boundaries of individual replies and have their linguistic correlatives in lexical oppositions, logical jumps and other phenomena which sometimes make an audience perceive associative rather than logical movement and structure. Referential instability of pronouns is an obvious form of semantic reversal: without any clear change of antecedent, we have second person pronouns referring first to Isabella, then to Angelo himself, and later to the 'cunning enemy', Satan. In the course of the speech, Angelo is himself the referent of first person singular and plural as well as second person pronouns. Such solecisms, in Renaissance rhetorical theory, *enallage*, emphasize the expressive or emotive function of this soliloquy. The series of antitheses: *tempter/tempted, violet/carrion, modesty/lightness, waste ground/sanctuary, foully/good, thieves/judges, cunning enemy/saint, strumpet/ maid, men/I* are logical oppostions which suggest the positive and negative poles of conflict and judgment in Angelo's mind and contribute to our sense of dialogic structure. But they are also evaluative, and their hyperbolic character serves to underscore their affective function.

Though careful attention to the sequence of developing ideas in the soliloquy reveals a logical framework for communicating rising emotion, Shakespeare creates the illusion of psychic process by subordinating strictly logical links between lexical units and exploiting instead associative links based on metaphor. The first line, motivated as I noted earlier by Isabella's 'Save your honour', which Angelo takes in quite a different sense from Isabella's intended formula of parting, initiates this associative movement. Angelo's shift via metaphor from temptation to corruption in lines 165–8 is communicated by a comparison of self to carrion and the description of its effect on a violet in the sun. Because of the sun's traditional association with God and reason, it is paradoxical that its beneficent rays corrupt. This paradox suggests to Angelo another related idea: if carrion corrupts the flower of the summer season, can it be, he wonders, that modesty rather than woman's lightness inspires lust? And as first Empson and later Lever pointed out, *season* is not only the time of year, summer, but also seasoning in food which acts as a preservative.[7]

Sense in line 169, which continues the pun on *sense* as sexual desire and *sense* as thought from the preceding interview, signals the double and opposed meanings of words and actions. Not only does the pun link the speech to its context by recalling Angelo's play on *sense* earlier in II, ii ('She speaks, and 'tis such sense/That my sense breeds with it.' 142–3), but it also exemplifies by its ambiguity the alternating semantic contexts characteristic of dialogue. Nor does logic motivate the following metaphor in which man's lust and its enactment is compared generally to military action, and topically to the immediate historical past of Tudor England in which Catholic property was desecrated.

Metaphor functions both as a mode of organization and as a means of projecting elsewhere beyond Angelo's immediate situation. The metaphorical language with its references to concrete reality – *violet, carrion, season, waste ground, sanctuary* – is not mimetic. It does not describe the external perceived reality these words denote so much as an internal state or imagined relation not justified by logic or reason; they are correlatives which communicate lust and its effects. In his discussion of metaphor and poetic language, the Prague linguist Jan Mukařovský suggests that 'we require of [a linguistic expression] something which is alien to the very essence and purpose of language, namely, that a sensorily perceptible linguistic symbol, the vehicle of *linguistic* meaning, become the vehicle of *psychic* meaning.'[8] We interpret these comparisons in terms of inexpressible psychic meaning rather than according to their concrete referential function. Angelo's metaphors are not so much speaking pictures as conveyors of his emotional state, his sense of corruption, violence and chaos. The desire he expresses, the repetition of phrases (lines 163, 164, 172, 173) and words (*desire*, lines 171, 174, 178); the use of such connotatively powerful words as *corrupt, sanctu-*

ary, enemy, saint; the series of strong caesuras, several marked additionally by adversatives, and finally the aposiopetic interjection 'ha' all serve to emphasize the intensity of Angelo's mental turmoil.

Angelo's avowal of desire in line 174 reminds him of his fraternity with Claudio: 'O, let her brother live!', he cries. What follows is a generic statement about thieves and judges which demonstrates the breakdown of difference which Angelo's desire for Isabella causes: by analogy Claudio is justified in his fornication with Juliet by Angelo's lust for Isabella. This generalization, with its implied comparison to Claudio, also makes ironic reference to Angelo's earlier self-judgment, 'When I that censure him do so offend,/Let mine own judgement pattern out my death,/And nothing come in partial' (II, i, 29–31). Angelo then jumps to speculation about his feelings: 'do I love her'. The shift from the implied analogy with Claudio to Angelo's question about love perhaps suggests a growing sympathy for Claudio and Juliet completely absent from Angelo's earlier speech and action.

Shakespeare also avoids narrative verb tenses in the first person which could create a distancing reportorial dimension in Angelo's speech. Instead the soliloquy depends on the generalizing present (*sins*, line 164, *do, does, corrupt*, lines 167–8, *have, steal*, lines 176–7, the verbs in lines 180 ff.). Tense changes in the speech signal the development of ideas already remarked upon, for example the shift from present to the optative 'may' in lines 168–9, or the repetition of 'dost' in lines 173–4, which links the two sentences rhetorically, but without any necessary logical connection. The oscillation between past and present, real and potential, specific and general is a distinctive mark of the freely associative language of interior monologue or self-address, both here and in other Shakespearean soliloquies.

The organization of Angelo's soliloquy as dialogue creates the dramatic illusion of a mind divided and persuades the audience of Angelo's inner conflict. His world has heretofore been organized by strictly differentiated and hierarchical judgments of self and world: woman's lightness, not modesty, generates lust; thieves, not judges, steal; desire of the good should be good desire. In his interchange with Isabella, Angelo discovers that such polar oppositions are false. Her virtue stimulates his lust, and that recognition stimulates his anxiety over discovering he is not different, but like other men. Shakespeare's careful presentation of Angelo's response to his discovery shows him to be a man of strong feelings and desires, quite different from the man 'whose blood/Is very snow-broth' described earlier by Lucio. This speech then is designed to present Angelo's mental life and persuade us emotionally of his recognition, struggle and judgment of his conflicting feelings.[9]

Though contemporary linguistics provides a vocabulary for analyzing Angelo's soliloquy and recognizing its affinities with dialogue, the student of literature inevitably asks how such strategies for representing mental life became available to an Elizabethan dramatist. One possibility immediately presents itself. Perhaps dialogue is actually a feature of mental life which Shakespeare transcribes from his own experience. But to argue so harks back to the old praise of Shakespeare's natural learning, for even if the dialogue of mental life is actually a phenomenon we can perceive by attending to our own process of thinking and reflection, Shakespeare must still be particularly adept and talented at rendering this experience in words. We find ourselves back where we started, not with an account of how Shakespeare carefully created the quality of an inner life in his characters, but with another question-begging claim for his natural ability to do so.

Instead, we might ask if this rhetoric of character derives from the educational training in rhetoric and the literary examples taught in the Elizabethan grammar school.[10] During the Renaissance, schoolboys and aspiring rhetoricians were required to interpret and enact fictitious situations both from outside, or narratively, and dramatically by speaking or writing in character. Rhetorical treatises and handbooks repeatedly emphasized the importance of what Aristotle in his discussion of metaphor in the *Rhetoric* called actualization (ἐνεργια), putting things before the eyes of the audience through created fictions. The handbooks themselves provided exercises to train the young student of rhetoric in the making of fictions. Perhaps the most popular in the Renaissance and the most widely used in England was the fourth-century grammarian Aphthonius' *Progymnasmata*, a series of exercises each accompanied by a model theme.[11] Aphthonius' *Progymnasmata* was translated into Latin ten times between 1507 and 1680 and printed one hundred and fourteen times, the greatest number of printings appearing between 1580 and 1630. In the eighteenth century, Saintsbury described Aphthonius as 'one of the most craftsmanlike crambooks that ever deserved the encomium of the epithet and the discredit of the noun'.

A look at the exercises themselves provides us with a clearer picture of what the Elizabethan student of rhetoric actually learned and practiced. The exercises are varied and arranged so as to increase in complexity, from simple paraphrase (*fabula*) to more complex forms of argumentation in which all the possible arguments on both sides of a question (*in utramque partem*) were marshalled to debate such topics as 'should a man marry?'. Most important for a young playwright, perhaps, was the exercise of impersonation or *ethopoeia*. Aphthonius divides this exercise into three categories, *ethopoeia* proper, in which the young scholar was required to speak from the point of view of a well-known historical or legendary figure; *eidolopoeia*, in which the student speaks in the person of someone dead; and *prosopopoeia*, in which the writer creates a wholly fictitious character. Aphthonius recognized the dramatic quality of these exercises, for he recommends Menander as the foremost exemplar of the form. His model for the figure consists of three invented first person monologues spoken by Niobe from the perspectives of present, past and future.

An essential technique in the creation of such characterizations was the imagined dialogue, an exercise the young scholars practiced in letter writing before moving on to the *progymnasmata*. Erasmus, whose works on education had enormous influence in the Elizabethan grammar school, recommends in his *De Conscribendis Epistolis* letters like

Ovid's *Heroides* to aid the student in imitating what particular persons might say in specific situations. The student learned to project himself into strange circumstances, to observe the decorum of person, audience and subject matter, and most importantly, to represent the psychology and mind of the imagined personage by attempting to respond to an imagined interlocutor. Character was created through dialogue both in legendary examples and in the examples Erasmus recommended from history and scripture. The descriptions of the exercises in impersonation which Erasmus and Aphthonius recommend and which were taught in Renaissance schools help to account for the tribute paid to Shakespeare by Pope, Hazlitt, Schlegel and others who praise Shakespeare's ability to put himself in the place of his characters, to imagine how they might think and feel in particular circumstances: in brief, to impersonate.

Aristotle defined rhetoric not as the art of persuasion, as did the sophists, but as the 'faculty of discovering the possible means of persuasion in reference to any subject whatever' (*Rhetoric*, I, ii, 1). It is not concerned therefore with the true, but with the probable, and its function is to deal with things uncertain, things for which we have no systematic rules. By creating fictions before the eyes of his audience, the rhetorician could persuade us of what could not be demonstrated. Rhetoric is the province of judicial and legislative debate, and inevitably of poetry, for both law and poetry are concerned with illusion, with *mimesis*. By creating in the mind of the auditor the verisimilar, the life-*like* rather than the real, the jurist convinces his audience. In later Latin works on rhetoric, the early anonymous *Ad Herennium*, Cicero's several works on rhetoric and oratory, and Quintilian's *Institutio*, this relationship between law and poetry is more fully developed.

All of these works draw their examples from literature. Cicero remarks upon the resemblance between the academic method of debate (*controversia* and *suasoria*) and the dialogues of tragedy and comedy (*De Natura Deorum*, 3.72–3). Quintilian recommends Menander and Euripides to the aspiring rhetorician (*Institutio* 10.1.69). He uses the *Orestes* to exemplify the way in which an argument or case depends on circumstances as the jurist presents them and on the effect of discourse. Though no general case can be made for matricide, a defense can be made for a specific person, Orestes, because in killing his mother he avenged his father. The use of the *Orestes* as an illustration, as well as the many other literary examples used by Cicero and others, imply that classical and Renaissance readers were familiar with fiction as a recognized means of analyzing questions of justice.[12] In fact, not only Quintilian, but the *Rhetorica ad Herennium*, Cicero's *De Inventione* and the derivative *Rhetores Latini Minores* take the majority of their examples from epic, drama and the fictional exercises of the *suasoria* and *controversia*. Literary fictions allowed for greater qualification through the manipulation of circumstances, and literary apologists of the Renaissance, most notably Sidney, take up this argument in the defense of poetry.

Most of the treatises and handbooks recommend three standard questions for organizing any controversy or debate: *sitne*, whether or not a given act was committed or situation obtains; *quid sit*, the definition of the act once admitted; and *quale sit*, the character or quality of the act once admitted and defined. Once the facts of a case are determined, the rhetorician must discover its *qualitates* by means of place logic, the categories of situation and kind, the how-and-in-what-state-of-mind the act was performed.[13] Cicero recognized the effectiveness of created fictions, what he called *personae* and *sermones*, in helping the audience see how something took place. Characters and speeches are always more convincing than mere statement or exposition, or the commonplaces of argument, for they foreground the *colores* or *qualitates*, those particulars which give the audience or reader a more complex view of character and incident than pure description can provide. In his discussion of law and Renaissance theories of art, Kantorowicz suggests that fiction was 'something artfully "created" by the art of the jurist; it was an achievement to his credit because fiction made manifest certain legal consequences which had been hidden before or which by nature did not exist'.[14]

In drama as in law the analysis and synthesis of qualities through speeches and episodes lead the audience to acquiesce emotionally to the plot of the play.[15] We must discover not only the place, time and occasion a given act was performed, not only who performed it, but how and in what state of mind. As Cicero admits in *De Partitione Oratoria*, 42–3, actions done because of emotional or mental disturbance cannot be defended in court, but they can be defended on the basis of qualitative issues in open debate, or we might add, on the public stage. And the greater the specificity with which the circumstances of a case or the mind of a character are investigated, the more the audience is implicated in motives and choices, questions of *qualitas*.[16]

Measure for Measure has often been likened to a judicial debate.[17] Immediately preceding Angelo's soliloquy, he and Isabella rigorously debate the relative claims of justice and mercy; indeed the entire play has sometimes been interpreted as a debate between justice and mercy. More recently, Joel Altman's work on Tudor drama in relation to rhetorical practice suggests that the ambivalence and multiplicity of perspectives characteristic of Renaissance English drama may be a product of a particular feature of rhetorical training, the practice of arguing *in utramque partem*, on both sides of the question.[18] Though *Measure for Measure* might be usefully approached as a philosophical *quaestio* which debates the opposing merits of justice and mercy, most readers would agree that character, rather than idea or abstraction, arrests the reader's or spectator's attention. Our response to the play's ambivalence derives as much from our responses to character as from logical arguments for any side. We do not question Isabella's refusal to give up her virginity, but her callous manner of doing so; we judge Angelo's behavior more by the quality of his mind as he discovers his desire than on the basis of his opinions or even his acts. Our response to the play is determined by the quality and circumstances of just and unjust, merciful and unmerciful, persons and acts.

By organizing Angelo's soliloquy as dialogue, Shakespeare represents the *qualitas* of his character's mind and thereby engages us more forcefully in Angelo's motives and choices for action. For the rhetorician, dialogue was a means of bringing out the latent issues in a larger issue by juxtaposing antithetical points of view. By contrasting the demands of Angelo's conscience with those of his desire, Shakespeare helps his audience to see more clearly Angelo's nature and his responsibility for his actions. We are led to admit that under certain circumstances, given other qualities, the tempter might indeed sin more than the tempted, and in III, i, as we listen to Isabella's shrill and vituperative repudiation of her brother's all too human desire to live, we find Isabella cast in Angelo's uncharitable role.

Interpretation depends on the occasion of utterance and its function in the larger dramatic organization of the play, not on psychological analysis. A typology of consciousness is only credible and significant if considered in relation to the larger structure of the comic plot. We need then to ask if we can discover by looking carefully at *Measure for Measure* an intersection of plot with this rhetoric of character which would help to explain the apparent contradiction between lifelikeness in characterization and conventional plots which has so long troubled critics of Shakespearean comedy.

2

Comic plot conventions in
Measure for Measure

Angelo's soliloquy occurs at that moment in *Measure for Measure* when his identity as judge or 'angel' is jeopardized by his desire for Isabella. Throughout Shakespeare's comic practice, we will find that this rhetoric of character or inner debate occurs at predictable moments in his comic plots of mistaken identity, and this conjunction of a rhetoric of consciousness with the mistaken identity plot produces in part our sense of complex character. It is important to observe, however, that this perception of the lifelike does not come from any necessary relation to reality, but only because such rhetoric generates an illusion of reality, what the French call *l'effet de réel*.[1] It is unimportant whether self-address is really a structure of mental life or psychic process, or whether people actually question their identities, or have identities at all; the point is that the validity of conventions is a function of our belief in them.[2]

Recent work on the realistic and naturalistic novels of the nineteenth century has demonstrated that conventions determine our perception of characters as realistic.[3] So also with the dramatic characters we call lifelike. Our perception of them as realistic is as determined by conventions as the mistaken identity plots in which they occur; in such plots, when a character questions his identity, or is mistaken for someone else, his suffering or confusion is represented through the rhetoric of consciousness. We perceive characters who use this rhetoric of self-address at those moments preceding the discovery in a mistaken identity plot as lifelike. In *Measure for Measure*, Angelo's disguise is a disguise of the mind rather than the body, but by juxtaposing Angelo's psychological predicament with the disguise plot of the Duke from romance, Shakespeare exploits both the psychological and external or physical dimensions of mistaken identity. The brief discussion of *Measure for Measure* which follows does not pretend to pass by the many shoals and reefs which endanger the critic's voyage through the play. Recent work on this comedy, both articles and several book-length studies, steers a fuller course through its dangerous waters.[4] I will endeavor to show only how *Measure for Measure* demonstrates particular features of Shakespeare's method of comic characterization.

If convention is a contract between artist and audience, as many have observed, we need to ask what are the binding rules or features of that contract.[5] What, for example, are the signals dramatists provide to make us read or perceive a particular dramatic convention in a particular way? What signals does Shakespeare provide to develop mistaken identity as a theme in *Measure for Measure* instead of simply a device for motivating plot?

In the Duke's first lines, he speaks of Angelo's assumption of his authority as a role. By applying the language of physical disguise and mistaken identity to the substitution of Angelo for the Duke, Shakespeare indicates to his audience the psychological dimension of the exchange. The Duke asks Escalus, 'What figure of us, think you, he will bear?'. Angelo is 'lent' his terror and 'dress't in his love. The Duke exhorts Angelo to use his virtues, makes allusion to the biblical parables of wasted virtue or skill, the candlestick, the talents and the line from Matthew, 'the tree is known by its fruit'.[6] The Duke calls upon Angelo to exercise his virtues in the

world, and this need for practiced virtue is emphasized by the
juxtaposition in the first scene of the Duke's descriptions of
Escalus and Angelo. Escalus is virtuous and wise, but his
virtue, unlike Angelo's, is proved:

> The nature of our people,
> Our city's institutions, and the terms
> For common justice, y'are as pregnant in
> As art and practice hath enriched any
> That we remember.
>
> (I, i, 9–13)

The Duke's exhortations to Angelo, however, declare that his
virtue remains to be tested, and his words to his proxy strike
the first note of the play's recurring theme of measure for
measure:

> nature never lends
> The smallest scruple of her excellence,
> But, like a thrifty goddess, she determines
> Herself the glory of a creditor,
> Both thanks and use.
>
> (I, i, 36–40)

The problem of measure for measure is, of course, endlessly
debated: should Angelo receive what he has attempted to
dispense? Can man who is by nature sinful judge a fellow
creature?

Shakespeare extends the language of substitution and
role-playing in this speech: to Angelo the Duke speaks of his
'part in him' and exhorts him 'In our remove, be thou at full
ourself'.[7] In exhorting him to practice his virtue, the Duke says
'Spirits are not finely touch'd/But to fine issues'. *Touch'd*
means to test gold or metal to assure its purity and to stamp or
imprint the metal to indicate it has been so tested. Angelo
continues the coining image; he is the metal, the Duke's role
as judge the face or imprint stamped upon him. Though these
lines are in part at least a conventional disclaimer, it is finally
true that Angelo's mettle is tested.[8] His formal request
becomes a test he has not imagined, and his method of
exercising justice indicates that initially he has no doubt of his
ability to judge. The Duke's response is simple and to the

point: 'No more evasion.' Angelo will no longer be allowed to evade the responsibilities of his virtue. The language of disguise and role-playing Shakespeare uses throughout this scene signals the double nature of mistaken identity.

Critics have found the Duke's actions, his substitution of Angelo for himself in this first act, inconsistent with the later avowal of his purpose to test Angelo (I, iii). They suggest that the Duke's knowledge of his proxy's dishonorable treatment of Mariana and the suspicions he voices to the friar in I, iii make his decision to entrust power to Angelo and his praise in the opening scene a serious textual problem.[9] Even this first scene, however, implies the Duke's later revealed purpose to test Angelo. The very biblical echoes noted above are also ambiguous. As Muir points out, the story from St Mark of the woman who had an issue of blood and who touched Jesus' garment so that she knew the 'virtue that went out of him' influences the phrasing of the Duke's speech.[10] Though in this passage 'issues' is positive, these lines echo the violence and questionable virtue of the biblical allusion and therefore prefigure the later action.

In the next scene we learn Claudio has been condemned to death for fornication. He gives several reasons for the harshness of Angelo's judgment, reasons which also suggest the discrepancy between Angelo's assumed role of judge and his true self, between his psychological disguise and his inner nature. In speculating whether it may be the newness of Angelo's position or his desire to establish authority which makes the Duke's deputy judge him harshly, Claudio uses the Renaissance commonplace that the 'body public be/A horse whereon the governor doth ride' (I, ii, 148–9). This Platonic metaphor is often used not only in political contexts, but as a figure for the difficulty of self-government. Later in the play when Angelo finds it impossible to govern his passion, he uses the figure to refer to himself. Claudio is uncertain 'Whether the tyranny be in his place,/Or in his eminence that fills it up'. Are Angelo's actions determined by his official position or by his inflated sense of his own eminence? Claudio claims that Angelo 'for a name/Now puts the drowsy and neglected act/Freshly on me: 'tis surely for a name' (I, ii, 158–60). Angelo is making a name for himself, as Claudio's repetition makes clear. We in the audience, warned in the first scene that Angelo is being tested, here share Claudio's tentative understanding of the deputy's motives for action.

The scene which follows between the Duke and the friar establishes the traditional disguise plot of romance which governs our response to the play and makes manifest what heretofore has only been suggested obliquely by metaphor and allusion: there is a discrepancy between Angelo's identity as judge and his true nature. The Duke has imposed his office on Angelo, 'Who may in th'ambush of my name strike home' (I, iii, 41). *Ambush* is always a negative word in Shakespearean usage which means 'to lurk' or 'to wait in hiding' Though Angelo will exercise justice protected by the Duke's name, his name or role will also 'ambush' Angelo, as his final lines imply: 'Hence shall we see/If power change purpose, what our seemers be.' In the first scene we understand that the Duke requires Angelo to exercise his virtue; in the next we have Claudio speculating on the reason for Angelo's harsh judgment; here the Duke reveals outright his purpose to test the angelic virtue Angelo's name suggests.

Act II, ii establishes the central structural and thematic irony of the play. Angelo has said to Escalus in justification of Claudio's condemnation, 'When I that censure him do so offend,/Let mine own judgement pattern out my death' (II, i, 29–30). Angelo will, in fact, so offend, and in her interview with Angelo, Isabella repeats this theme. Angelo believes himself immune, safe from the sin committed by Claudio; Isabella recognizes his inflated self confidence:

> But man, proud man,
> Dress'd in a little brief authority,
> Most ignorant of what he's most assur'd –
> His glassy essence – like an angry ape
> Plays such fantastic tricks before high heaven
> As makes the angels weep; who, with our spleens,
> Would all themselves laugh mortal.
>
> (II, ii, 118–24)

The imagery of clothing in these lines continues the language of role-playing: power is a disguise man puts on which hides his 'glassy essence', his pure self, the center of his being which is transparent because there is no farther to look, no hidden recess. Lever glosses this line as 'most ignorant of his own spiritual entity' and quotes J. V. Cunningham who, from other Shakespearen usage, interprets man's essence as his 'intellectual soul, which is an image of God, and hence glassy for it mirrors God'.[11] For Angelo the power represented by the Duke's role prevents self-knowledge as truly as the mistaken identities involving twins, lost children and love potions prevent understanding in the early comedies. The activity Isabella associates with this misunderstanding of self is acting a part: man is like an angry ape, aping God's judgment before heaven, playing fantastic tricks. Her lines are another version of Jaques' 'all the world's a stage', but more painful and accusing. They reduce man's play-acting to that of a beast by calling attention not simply to his absurdity as a man, as Jaques does, but to the grotesque posturing of his bestial nature. Isabella's comparison of stern judge to gnarled oak split by heaven's 'sharp and sulphurous bolt' is a Renaissance commonplace for justice and mercy. Her progression from 'giant' (line 109), to 'great man' (line 111), to 'petty officer' (line 113), to 'man' (line 118), to 'angry ape' (line 121) signals the degeneration of those who mimic God's justice rather than his mercy.

In her next long speech, Isabella moves from the impersonal man to the personal: 'Go to your bosom,/Knock there, and ask your heart what it doth know/ That's like my brother's fault' (II, ii, 137–9). Ironically, as his soliloquy demonstrates, Angelo heeds her words and discovers his own desire: 'She speaks, and 'tis such sense/That my sense breeds with it' (II, ii, 142–3). The pun on *sense* here is doubly appropriate: words seem as surely as do men, and it is this kind of word-play which characterizes their second meeting, creating its ironies and cross-purposes.[12] Angelo believes he controls completely his human feeling and passion; the Duke's authority encourages him to live out this identity and he finds it wanting. His confidence in his immunity to temptation makes recognizing his human feeling for Isabella so difficult, and the soliloquy which ends the scene represents that struggle.[13]

In terms of its larger function in the play the soliloquy reveals what till now has only been prophecy and foreshadowing: Angelo, who has condemned Claudio to death for a natural sexual lapse, will then repeat the lapse, compound his crime and be judged for it. And it is worth remembering that Shakespeare has the Duke arrange with great nicety that Angelo's sexual activity duplicate that for which he condemned Claudio.

In his soliloquy at II, iv, Angelo makes explicit for the first time this troubling realization of the difference between inner and outer: Angelo's lust for Isabella awakens not only his desire for sensual experience, but also his pride. He recognizes that his position as judge and his 'gravity' (II, iv, 9) are external attributes: they are a 'case' and 'habit' (line 13). He addresses his 'place' and 'form' in the second person, as if they were independent. These lines end with the most precise paradox describing Angelo yet, that paradox which focuses on the irony of his name, the 'good angel on the devil's horn' (II, iv, 16). In this speech Angelo admits his human propensity for sin. His repression of desire finds release, and like Plato's horse, it cannot be restrained. His words 'now I give my sensual race the rein' (line 159) echo Claudio's language describing Angelo's actions in I, iii.

The metaphor of disguise which extends our understanding of mistaken identity in the play is continued in the second meeting between Angelo and Isabella; she vehemently attacks his seeming while he tries to make her understand his 'sense'. Angelo means for his words to have one construction, but Isabella understands them in another: the meaning of language is determined by the auditor as surely as by the speaker, by the total speech act, and irony is created by the failure of one aspect of that act, the hearer's inability to understand Angelo's proposition. Words wear disguises as surely as do men; language and identity are relative, dependent at least in part on the world outside as well as the self within.

Shakespeare further complicates the psychological disguise plot of *Measure for Measure* by the series of substitutions or doublings he works out in the play. Angelo's reciprocal relation to the Duke is established through the action itself, but also by the metaphor of imprinting in the first scene, and by the repeated references to Angelo as his deputy; his relationship to Claudio is established by his desire for Isabella, but he is also linked to Isabella herself throughout the play.[14] As Angelo's lines at II, ii suggest, Isabella is like him, a kind of double: 'O cunning enemy, that, to catch a saint,/With saints dost bait thy hook!' Nor is this the first link Shakespeare makes between Isabella and Angelo. In her first scene she asks of the nun 'a more strict restraint' (I, iv, 4), words which inevitably recall the Duke's description of Angelo in the immediately preceding scene, 'A man of stricture and firm abstinence'. L. C. Knights has pointed out that 'the unfamiliarity of the world *stricture* ensures that its derivation from *stringere*, to bind together or strain, shall contribute to the meaning of the line', but he fails to remark the adjectival form used by Isabella in the immediately following scene.[15] Both Angelo and Isabella self-consciously abstain from contact with the opposite sex; both seek restraint and repress the demands of sexual difference and desire. And it is exactly their doubleness, their seeming lack of difference, which makes Angelo desire Isabella, as he admits in his soliloquy.

In IV, iv, when Angelo learns that the Duke is returning by way of a royal progress, his language reflects the play's controlling metaphor of disguise: the Duke's deed 'unshapes' him, both literally by taking away his power and identity as judge, and figuratively by disturbing his mind with remorse. In the final act, there is not one discovery, but three. The Duke is revealed, and his discovery, like that of the *virgo* or of the existence of twins, puts the action to rights. Angelo is exposed; he confesses to his crimes in religious language ('confession', 'grace', 'power divine', 'passes') which Shakespeare uses to mark the movement from sin to repentance characteristic of the romances with which this play is so often linked. Finally, Isabella herself discovers the true mercy for which she argued in her earlier interview with Angelo. Having undergone a figurative 'repair i' the dark' in facing the public shame of accusing Angelo, at Mariana's behest Isabella refuses the Duke's call for vengeance and instead begs for Angelo's life. In doing so she transcends the reciprocal violence of vengeance Claudio's supposed death initiates and which Angelo's death would continue. The title of the play and the series of equivalences which it sets up and insists upon are not borne out in the final act. Instead, difference is re-established by the return of hierarchy in the person of the Duke and by Isabella's merciful and ritual pleading on Angelo's behalf.[16]

This brief discussion of the play suggests some of the ways Shakespeare creates complex comic characters within the confines of a mistaken identity plot. Soliloquies and monologic fragments which manifest a rhetoric of consciousness occur at predictable moments in comic plots of mistaken identity when a character's identity is questioned and he finds himself adrift, cut loose from his normal bearings and without a guide. This rhetoric represents a divided mind through particular features which the audience perceives as signs of psychological complexity and realism. The movement, from ignorance through confusion to discovery, of the typical mistaken identity plot, when joined to this rhetoric of consciousness, creates the illusion of development and change which we identify with Shakespeare's greatness as a dramatist. In *Measure for Measure*, the language of disguise and role-playing signals the psychological resonance of its mistaken identity plot of complex substitutions and exchanges.

Convention may be defined as a regularity of behavior produced by a system of expectations.[17] By such a definition, two conventions of comic plots are the mental error or mistaken identity which creates the dramatic conflict, and the *anagnorisis* or discovery which Aristotle tells us in the *Poetics* every good plot requires. Mistaken identity is of two sorts: first, errors caused by ignorance or by the deliberate concealment of some fact (the identity of Oedipus' parents, the origins of the Antipholi in *The Comedy of Errors*, or Don John's duping of Claudio in *Much Ado*); and secondly, psychological errors caused by the mistakes a character makes about himself, his judgment or his inner nature (Lear's rejection of Cordelia or Angelo's identity as 'angel'). Comic dramatists often combine these two types of error: ignorance of a simple fact provokes a character to action which makes him recognize his true nature and the mistakes he has made about it. This recognition or discovery leads, in turn, to comic enlightenment or the exposure of folly.[18]

In any given plot, misapprehension or mistaken identity always produces a system of expectations which can only be satisfied by discovery, the transition from ignorance to knowledge which necessarily involves a reversal of fortune. Mistaken identity is a convention of comedy in so far as the repeated act of viewing plays makes the audience expect that plots will behave in a certain way, for no matter how we arrange the various possibilities a mistake or error offers, we must always have the discovery in order to resolve a given plot. Discovery, we might say, is the comic convention *par excellence*.

Shakespeare learned the conventions he uses for constructing comic plots and realistic characters from his rhetorical training in the Elizabethan grammar school. But even a brief look at the sources of that training suggests that Renaissance educators and students inherited both their tools and their literary examples from the ancients. We need to turn then to the earliest practitioners of comedy themselves to discover Shakespeare's dramatic precedents for presenting character.

3

Menander and
New Comedy

Shakespeare's relation to his classical predecessors has been
studied and pondered from a multiplicity of angles, from the
perspective of specific borrowings and analogues in the work of
Baldwin, Bullough and others, to the structural and thematic
relationships suggested by Barber and more recently Leo
Salingar and Robert Weimann. Inquiry into the influence of
New Comedy on Shakespeare has generally fallen into two
major areas: Saturnalia or the festive element which Barber so
cogently explored in *Shakespeare's Festive Comedy*, and stock
characterization and plot which Bernard Knox delineated in
his classic essay on *The Tempest* and ancient comedy.[1] Though
Salingar has contributed astute readings of often ignored
classical plays, and Weimann has assembled often overlooked
popular source materials, both remain essentially within the
parameters defined by earlier scholars. Both give short shrift to
Menander and the New Comic tradition he represents. Careful
reading of the extant plays of Menander as well as his Roman
imitators, however, suggests another field of comparison

which serves to illuminate both the nature of Shakespeare's debt to the earliest practitioners of comedy and his own originality.

Menander's fame throughout antiquity was immense. The Greek critic Aristophanes of Byzantium characterized Menander's reputation when he wondered which of the two, life or Menander, copied the other. Quintilian claimed that the careful study of Menander alone would be sufficient to train the perfect orator; Propertius, Ovid and Ausonius refer to him as the chief poet of love. Ancient writers quote him again and again, and the constant allusions to his name and reputation show that he was widely regarded as the finest comic playwright of Greece. The dearth of extant texts of Menander's plays, and more importantly, the twentieth-century preoccupation with the origins of drama and the popular tradition represented by Aristophanes and Old Comedy, account for the decline in his reputation.

We are uncertain when the plays of Menander were lost. As late as the fifth century, Sidonius Apollinaris laid Menander's *Epitrepontes* and Terence's similarly plotted *Hecyra* before his son in one of the earliest examples of the comparative method.[2] By the middle ages, however, Menander existed only in fragments and in scattered allusions which testify to his continued reputation. In the sixteenth century, Menander was available in a collection of fragments published in Paris in 1553 in two editions, both in Greek, one with facing Latin text. But for the Renaissance, the most eminent comic dramatist of antiquity was essentially a poet without a text. His influence on Renaissance comedy is not direct; it comes into the period by way of hellenistic romance which was influenced by Euripides and New Comedy; by way of Roman comedy and its vernacular imitations; and through rhetorical handbooks which recommended New Comic strategies of characterization.[3]

Comic stereotypes evolved out of dramatic and oratorical traditions and were eventually codified first in Aristotle's discussion of types in the *Rhetoric* and the *Ethics*, and later by Theophrastus, the teacher of Menander, and by Cicero.

Aristotle describes a series of men – old, young, wealthy, dissolute – and the attributes appropriate to each in generalized terms according to their habits, ages and fortunes; Theophrastus bases his *Characters*, published three years after the production of Menander's first comedy, on observations of detail. For example, he describes three different misers, each with different traits and details of behavior. The types commonly associated with comedy, the braggart, the flatterer, the young lover, the old man, are thought to come into the Renaissance from Aristotle, Theophrastus, Cicero and Quintilian, as well as from the Roman dramatists.

Although critics have most often cited types as the major difference between Shakespearean and New Comic characterization, type characterization need not preclude change or character development.[4] We all know that in most of Shakespeare's comedies, the self-deceived undergo changes which are integral to the movement of the plot. Shakespeare is traditionally opposed in this respect to the ancients and to Jonson, that most classical of Renaissance playwrights, in whose plays ignorance and self-deception function to render the victim susceptible to intrigue perpetrated by other characters and to expose his folly, but are not designed to lead to a change in character. As Salingar puts it, 'the most general working rule ... in New Comedy is that there should be confusion over someone's identity, not primarily his psychological identity, his inner self, but his birth, his original name and status'.[5] But in Menander there is abundant evidence that type characters break the bonds of their stereotypes, grow and change. Menander consistently uses external mistakes and errors to occasion just that kind of psychological or internal change which Salingar and others attribute only to Shakespeare. Classicists have long recognized Menander's interest in character and his serious intentions.[6] The comedies of Menander reveal a long tradition of using the conventional device of mistaken identity to develop character and dramatize the theme of self-knowledge on the New Comic stage.

Recent discoveries of papyri in Egypt now afford us one complete play of Menander and substantial portions of five others. We know the *Dyskolus* to be an early play because it won first prize at the dramatic festival of Lenaea in 316 BC; the *Perikeiromene* and the *Epitrepontes* are assigned to his mature period. The three plays employ the same techniques for dramatizing psychological change and development and are representative of Menander's preoccupation with character.

Menander's *Dyskolus* or *The Grouch* deals almost exclusively with psychological or inner mistaken identity. There are no lost children, no birth tokens, no twins. As Pan reports in the prologue, Knemon, the grouch of the title, has false assumptions about himself and the world. He is the *senex iratus par excellence*; his grouchiness is the expression of his misanthropy. Though the play does involve the marriage of Knemon's daughter to a young lover, its real business is to educate Knemon by exposing the limits of the cynic philosophy of self-sufficiency.[7] When the play opens, he has rejected everyone – friends, neighbors, wife, stepson – believing them to be self-interested. He thinks that by doing so he can be wholly self-sufficient. The major action of the play involves his fall into a well, a parodic descent into the underworld, from which he is saved by the very person he has rejected most unfairly, his stepson. Here, as he will in later plays, Menander uses the motif of 'losing to find', for in the well where he almost loses his life, Knemon finds himself.

When he emerges, his stepson Gorgias tells Knemon that his experience is similar to his self-imposed isolation and misanthropy. His stepfather, Gorgias says, has been living in that same darkness, but in psychological rather than physical terms. The well is the physical embodiment of his psychological state, and physical suffering is the means of his psychological release. Gorgias' generous action disproves Knemon's view of the world; therefore, Knemon acknowledges him as his son. The old man's self-questioning is objectified in his suffering in the well, and by his own admission, it leads him to greater self-knowledge. The soliloquy which follows was probably spoken from the *ekkylema* or rolling platform, a conventional device belonging to tragedy.[8]

> I was, it seems, wrong in one regard: Thinking that I alone of all was truly self-sufficient and would never be in need of anyone. But now that I have seen that the end of life is sudden and unforeseen, I find I was mistaken. One needs a person who will help one, who will be at one's side. But, by Hephaestus! my mind was corrupted when I saw how people lived, always calculating for their own advantage. I thought that nobody could be well disposed to anybody else. This is what stood in my way. Now, at last, one person, Gorgias, has provided the proof, by doing what only the noblest man would do. Though I would not allow him to come to my door, never helped him in the slightest, never addressed or spoke him a friendly word, he saved my life. And then he could have said, and rightly, 'Since you do not let me come near, I do not come near; you have not been useful to us, neither am I to you now!' What is it, my boy? Whether I die now (and I think I shall, I seem to be in a bad way) or live on, I make you my son. Therefore consider everything I chance to have your own.[9]

Knemon's monologue presents a man questioning his past assumptions and changed by his recent experience. Though very different from Angelo's soliloquy, it displays some of the features of dialogue used to represent the inner life. Knemon makes his speech before an audience consisting of Gorgias and others, yet not until the final lines does he speak directly to his stepson. Instead, he muses aloud about his past behavior and refers to Gorgias in the third person. The old man hypothesizes what 'anyone else in his [Gorgias'] place would have said'. The invented interchange with a hypothetical interlocutor establishes the I/you dichotomy of dialogue; that 'anyone else' we understand to be Knemon himself who recounts what he would have felt and said had he found himself in Gorgias' predicament. Menander's emphasis on error dispelled by the stepson testifies to his interest in educating Knemon, for the misanthropist's fall into the well leads to the re-establishment of familial and social relationships which he has heretofore denied. In the remainder of the play the servants whom he has earlier harassed harass him and finally drive him to take part in the festivities which mark the final reconciliation.

The *Perikeiromene* or *She Who Was Shorn*, usually dated late fourth century BC, is another example of how Menander uses mistaken identity not as a simple plot device, but to develop his characters. Though the play is based on a typical plot involving twins, the dramatic interest is focused on the psychology of Glycera, the female twin, and her husband, Polemon. Menander emphasizes Polemon's growth from frenzied jealous lover to guilt-ridden, frightened man to beloved and forgiven husband, and Glycera's role as agent of his reformation.

But the most interesting play of Menander's we possess is the *Epitrepontes* or *The Arbitration*, acknowledged in antiquity and by modern commentators as one of Menander's finest. It opens as the protagonist Charisios returns from a long journey and discovers that while he was away, his wife Pamphile, having been raped before their marriage at a religious festival, has had a child. He rejects her, moves out, takes a mistress, and determines to lead a dissolute life in retaliation for her defilement. The child is discovered with identifying birth tokens, in this case the ring which Pamphile pulled from her assailant's hand. The ring turns out to be Charisios'; he was his wife's unknown assailant and is, of course, the father of the child. As the plot summary suggests, Menander's play does not conform with the often repeated paradigms of New Comedy; though the situation is domestic, it does not involve a young man who thwarts parental authority in attempting to win a girl. The complications of plot are only a pretext for the real business of the play: Charisios' recognition of his own guilt, his confrontation of the fact that he committed rape but rejected his wife merely for being the victim of such a crime.

More important than any mistaken identity is his discovery of Pamphile's continued loyalty. When her father Smikrines, angry at his son-in-law's unreasonable and extravagant behavior, attempts to persuade his daughter to reject her husband, Charisios overhears her refusal to leave him. For Menander, the important discovery for his protagonist is that his wife, whom he has rejected for being the victim of a crime he himself has committed, refuses to obey her father and remains loyal to her husband. His discovery of her devotion prompts this confrontation with himself which was evidently Menander's intention, a conclusion we make because he dramatizes Charisios' reaction to his wife's loyalty, not his discovery of his own paternity, nor his discovery that his wife is the mother of his child. Mistaken identity is not simply a plot device, but the means for Charisios' self-confrontation.

The scene begins with a monologue spoken by the servant in which he describes Charisios' response to the conversation between Pamphile and her father. Charisios, we are told, lost his mind, his color changed, his eyes were bloodshot, and he hit himself over the head. Onesimos even reports Charisios' condemning himself, recognizing his ironic identity with his wife's situation:

> 'I'm the miscreant! I'm the one that did such a thing! I myself am the father of a bastard child! Yet I never had nor gave her a fraction of forgiveness in her misfortune over these same matters! A pitiless barbarian!' (p. 123)[10]

By having Onesimos' description of his master's reaction to the discovery precede Charisios' own speech, Menander shifts the dramatic emphasis from the moment of discovery itself to its effect on Charisios' character. His soliloquy demonstrates his acknowledgement of guilt and increased self-understanding:

> A man without feelings, always looking to his reputation, always discriminating between the fine act and the disgraceful, a man untouched by vice, himself blameless in his mode of life – oh, well and altogether fittingly the divine power has dealt with me! Here and now it has revealed me. 'O thrice a wretch, though only a man, you puff yourself up and talk big. Yet you cannot endure your wife's unwilled misfortune. But I will show you fallen into similar straits. She will treat you kindly then, though you dishonor her now. And you will be shown all at once as an unfortunate and clumsy fool! Indeed she said to her father then quite what you were

thinking – oh yes! That she had become the partner of your life, that it wasn't right for her to shun an adventitious misfortune. But you were such a high-minded fellow!' [Six lines lost] But what is her father to me? I'll say directly to him, 'Don't give me trouble, Smikrines. My wife is not going to leave me. Why harass and pressure Pamphile?'. (p. 124)[11]

Classicists generally agree that the conventions of self-absorption on stage have more in common with Euripidean tragedy than with Aristophanic comedy.[12] In an invented divine rebuke, Charisios imagines a supernatural power addressing him, condemning his hypocrisy. Robert Weimann claims that this soliloquy 'seems so out of context and dramatically inappropriate that it is easily turned to comic effect ... the illusion of not being overheard still must have seemed so weak that it could be comically dismissed'.[13] In the standard commentary on this text, however, the noted classicist E. H. Sandbach points out that τὸ δαιμόνιον is a vague term meaning 'supernatural power' not found elsewhere in Menander or the remains of New Comedy.[14] The phrase is not banal, but elevates the speech above the level of the comic everyday, as does the rhetorical device of *prosopopoeia*. Here and elsewhere, Menander uses tragic diction, as E. W. Handley has observed, not for its purely laughable or satiric possibilities as does Aristophanes, but to gain an extra dimension for his comic action by referring it implicitly to the classical standard of tragedy.[15] Not only modern critics, but late classical, medieval and Renaissance commentators as well, recognized this tragic dimension in Menander's comedy. Donatus, for example, several times notes that Terence diverges from Menander lest his play should rise up into tragedy.

The rhetorical figure *prosopopoeia* not only contributes to the seriousness of the speech, but more importantly allows for the kind of self-address we find Shakespeare using later over and over again throughout the comedies and tragedies whenever a character questions his identity.[16] Aphthonius' popular rhetoric, we should remember, recommended the figure for creating character and praises Menander as its best practitioner. *Prosopon* is a compound form of the preposition *pros* (in front of), and *opon* (face), and therefore means not simply 'person' or 'face' but 'mask', προσωπεῖον. In the most literal sense the word means 'to make or create a mask': *prosopopoeia* is a figure of impersonation, and it is translated as such by the Renaissance figurists. The verbal form in Greek means both 'to personify' and 'to dramatize a dialogue'. In sixteenth-century rhetorical handbooks, the figure was often associated with *dialogisimus*. The wearer of a mask is projected beyond his personal identity to become 'other' as happens to Charisios in this scene – he loses his identity and is transformed by assuming a rhetorical mask which enables him to address himself. His speech, both as reported and as dramatized, manifests those features which reappear characteristically in comedies of mistaken identity at moments of dramatic tension, usually preceding or during the scene of comic discovery. First we find self-address through the objectification of self in second-person self-reference, here through the rhetorical figure, *prosopopoeia*, for the supernatural power with whom Charisios converses plays the role of his conscience. Next, Menander uses rhetorical questions (lines 918–20, 928–31) to extend the I/you dichotomy and he relates the speaker firmly to the material situation (cf. lines 908 ff.). Missing from Charisios' soliloquy are the enriching nuances created by metaphor so important to Angelo's speech and to our sense of his inner life. *Prosopopoeia*, though an effective means of creating inner dialogue, is less subtle than Shakespeare's more internalized dialogue with self in *Measure for Measure* II, ii, 162–87. Nevertheless, Charisios, like Angelo, must lose himself to find his true identity.

In his study of the popular tradition, Weimann complains that Menander and the New Comic dramatists, instead of considering themselves as 'guardians of and sharers in public interests', were paid entertainers, often strangers, like Diphilos and Philemon, to cities where their plays were performed.[17] This changed relation to theatrical practice along with political changes in Greek social life such as the discontinuation of the *theorikon* – the subsidy which enabled all citizens to attend the public theatres – brought about a widening gulf between the actor and his audience. Weimann views the gulf and New Comedy in general as a decline from the popular tradition of Aristophanes.

But as he himself points out, this separation of actor and audience also brought about an 'increasing dramatic illusion of verisimilitude' which led to the development of fictive settings and the so-called fourth wall. As the theatrical scene achieved a higher level of representation, the actors submitted to new conventions of illusion and impersonation, particularly the increased use of soliloquy spoken not to the audience, but to the self, a dialogue which the audience overhears from the other side of the fourth wall.[18]

Nevertheless, anti-realistic features characteristic of Old Comedy such as masks continued to be employed by New Comic dramatists. The custom of wearing masks provides an interesting perspective on mistaken identity in Menander's plays. T. B. L. Webster points out that

> in the recognition plays the audience would know as soon
> as they saw the girl that she was going to be recognized as a
> citizen whatever might be her momentary status, and the
> mask would confirm the hint given in the prologue
> speech.[19]

The masks, like the prologues which explain the errors, emphasize the irony on which so many of these plays are built by constantly reminding the audience, even in moments of extreme crisis, of the true identity of the characters. What kind of mask is given to a character who comes to some radical realization about himself in the course of the play – Knemon in the *Dyskolus* or Charisios in the *Epitrepontes*? L. A. Post suggests that Charisios may have been presented in a new mask as a reformed character in the final scenes, but he may have retained his earlier mask, an ironic reminder to the audience of his double self.[20]

As Sidonius long ago recognized, the *Epitrepontes* and Terence's *Hecyra* or *The Mother-in-law* share the same central plot device, a rape which results in the birth of a child, the repudiation of a wife, and a central irony, that the husband was his wife's unknown assailant. Terence, however, handles the plot quite differently, in ways which serve to illuminate Menander's intentions to dramatize Charisios' development and psychological change. Like Pamphile in Menander's play, Terence's Philumena is a loving, dutiful and patient wife. The young husband, Pamphilus, has a history of dissipation, but obeys his father in marrying. Here the similarities end. When Terence's play opens, Philumena has returned to her parents' house. The cause of her return, her pregnancy, is a secret not only from the other characters, but from us in the audience as well. The young husband's mother is blamed for Philumena's departure, because, as Terence's title indicates, he bases his play on one of the oldest clichés in the world, the familial problems which marriage creates: the conflicting loyalties of son to mother, son to wife, mother to daughter, and father to son. The courtesan Bacchis, whom Pamphilus once loved, discovers he was his wife's assailant and has Pamphilus' servant tell him of the discovery in the final scene. Pamphilus is overjoyed and simply returns to his wife with no avowals of guilt or self-accusation. With his usual selfishness, he even manages to keep the news of his crime from his father. Character development and self-knowledge are not a part of Terence's dramatic strategy in the *Hecyra*.

In most of Shakespeare's comedies, however, as in Menander's, the self-deceived undergo changes which are integral to the movement of the plot. In both the comedies and the tragedies, the ignorant or self-deceived are the protagonists, the characters whose fates concern us. Both playwrights use the comic soliloquy with its characteristic features of dialogue to dramatize character development. By contrast, in Jonsonian and much Roman comedy, ignorance and self-deception function to render the victim susceptible to intrigue perpetrated by other characters, and also to expose his folly, but are not designed to effect a change in character.

Plautus and Terence did, however, imitate Menander and the New Comic dramatists. We need to turn now to Latin comedy and its use of soliloquy and mistaken identity to examine the ways in which these traditions for representing character development were carried on and passed eventually into the Renaissance.

4

Plautus and Terence

Menander uses mistaken identity plots and the comic soliloquy to portray a learning process in which a character comes
better to understand himself, his situation, and his responsibility for his actions. Plautus uses word-play, rhythm, spectacle and
parody to make comic capital of the theme of self-knowledge.
His plays and their Renaissance adaptations demonstrate
that Plautus and his imitators recognized the thematic
importance of mistaken identity and the rhetoric of consciousness. But because he uses the mistaken identity plot and the set
speech for comic purposes, critics have often ignored the
Plautine model. Yet it provided an important channel of
influence for New Comic strategies of rendering the inner life
and movement toward self-knowledge of comic characters.[1]

Plautus and Terence represent the chief dramatic tradition
from which Renaissance comedy sprang. During the middle
ages Terence was far more popular and widely read than
Plautus both for his style and moral tone. The Renaissance
interest in Plautus and Latin comedy can be traced to the

arrival of Cusanus at Rome in 1429 with a manuscript containing sixteen Plautine comedies, twelve of which had been lost for centuries, and to the discovery of a manuscript of Donatus' commentary at Mayence in 1433. Throughout the late fifteenth century, Plautus was performed in Latin and in vernacular translations in Italy and elsewhere. These productions were mounted not only at courts, but in the academies and schools. Plautus' plays inspired Ariosto's early comedies, and influenced subsequent Renaissance comic practice throughout Europe. We thus need to begin by looking at several Plautine comedies to discover how he uses the rhetoric of consciousness for comic effect.

Plautus' *Amphitryo* opens with a prologue spoken by Mercury in which he explains the argument – Jupiter has impersonated Amphitryo in order to seduce Alcmena, and Mercury has impersonated Amphitryo's slave Sosia to help his father. On the last night before the real Amphitryo's victorious return from war, Jupiter has asked Night to extend her hours to permit him extra pleasure. The play proper opens on the real Sosia approaching his master's house with Mercury watching and commenting from the side. Sosia has been commissioned by his master to tell Alcmena of his victory at war and of his impending return. The scene begins in characteristically Plautine fashion with Sosia's invented comic boast about his brave behavior in battle juxtaposed against his actual pusillanimity when he sees Mercury standing before the doors of Amphitryo's house. Within the comic framework of the play, the meeting between Sosia and Mercury is a confrontation of Sosia with Sosia, a corporeal encounter of self with self.

This scene was so influential a representation of mistaken identity and doubling that both the Italians and the French have taken the proper name *Sosia* or *Sosie* as a noun meaning 'double' or 'twin'. Many modern critics have been tempted to philosophize about this scene, to view it as 'the problem of everyman; that is, ultimately, he is a stranger to himself'.[2] But this scene parodies as well as dramatizes an existential problem. Plautus has taken what was a serious theme in Greek drama and New Comedy and parodied it in part through the comic business of contrasting Sosia's boasts with his cowardly behavior, but more importantly by parodying the rhetoric of consciousness which Menander had used for more serious purposes.

In the interchange with Mercury Sosia poses himself a series of rhetorical questions (lines 402 ff., 455 ff.) and appeals to his past experience and common sense to assert his identity:

> nonne hac noctu nostra navis (huc) ex portu Persico
> venit, quae me advexit? non me huc erus misit meus?
> nonne ego nunc sto ante aedis nostras? non mi est lanterna
>   in manu?
> non loquor? non vigilo? nonne hic homo modo me pugnis
>   contudit?
>
> (lines 404–8)

> Didn't our ship arrive this very night from Perse Harbour, and
> me on it? Didn't my master send me here? Aren't I standing
> in front of our own house? Aren't I carrying this lantern?
> Isn't this me speaking? Am I awake? Hasn't this fellow beaten
> me black and blue? (p. 244)[3]

Both he and Mercury, and later Amphitryo, accuse him of madness and dreaming. Sosia is convinced he has lost himself, literally: 'ubi ego perii? ubi immutatus sum? ubi ego formam perdidi?/an egomet me illic reliqui, si forte oblitus fui?' (lines 456–7). ('Where did I lose myself? Where was I translated? Where did I shed my skin? Have I gone and left myself at the harbour by mistake?' p. 246). Later in an absurd conversation with his master, he asserts 'sum profecto et hic et illic' (line 594) ('I am here and there'). He is driven to imagine himself a twin: 'geminus Sosia hic factust tibi'. His speech here is reminiscent of monologues of discovery which we find so often at the close of comedies of mistaken identity:

> Sosiam servom tuom
> praeter me alterum, inquam, adveniens faciam ut offendas domi,
> Davo prognatum patre eodem quo ego sum, forma, aetate item
> qua ego sum. quid opust verbis? geminus Sosia hic factust tibi.
>
> (lines 612–15)

> I bet you anything you like, when you open that door you'll find

another slave Sosia; son of my father Davus; same age as
me; same face, same everything. Well that explains it,
doesn't it? You've got twins! (p. 253)

There is, of course, more of the ridiculous than the pathetic in
Sosia's plight; nevertheless the rhetorical devices Plautus uses
suggest both a psychological and mythical dilemma – the
rivalry of twinship or doubles and the confrontation of self
with self.

Renaissance adapters of Plautus and Latin comedy recognized and exploited the comic possibilities of this rhetoric of
consciousness. Early in the scene between master and slave,
Amphitryo asks Sosia

> tune id dicere audes, quod nemo umquam homo antehac
> vidit nec potest fieri, tempore uno
> homo idem duobus locis ut simul sit?
>
> (lines 566–8)

> Have you the face to tell me something no one has ever seen on
> this earth and never will – one man in two places at the same time?
> (p. 251)

The Renaissance Protestant adapter used these two scenes to
attack the doctrine of transubstantiation. In the interlude *Jack
Juggler* he parodies the motif of self-reference by multiplying
the pronouns. The Sosia figure, Jack Careaway, uses both the
first and third person to refer to himself:

> And is not he-I an unkind knave,
> That woll no more pity on my self have?
> Here may you see evidently, i-wis,
> That in him-me no drop of honesty is.[4]

Both Plautus and his English adapter understand the comic
potential of such a meeting; both are parodying the problem of
the divided self. Neither uses the device to force his character
to face any of the psychological implications which confrontation with self raises, and neither shows characters who change
and develop. Whether for purposes of comic absurdity or
mocking religious dogma, this rhetoric of the divided self was
available to Renaissance comic playwrights, to be exploited

not only for its comic possibilities, but, as we shall see, for its potential as a means of characterization.

We should look also at Plautus' *Pseudolus*, said by Cicero, who greatly admired it, to be the playwright's own favorite. The *Pseudolus* is larded with soliloquies spoken by the trickster slave in which we find the rhetoric of consciousness characteristic of complex comic characters. Plautus' slaves, as is well known, are intriguers, creators opposed to the irascible masters and crooks who represent a conservative, property-conscious society. Their deceits, which are never punished ensure the triumph of a less rigid social order, usually represented by an erotic relationship. They are, therefore, morally positive within the world in which they operate, which is why, despite continual threats of punishment, Plautine slaves are never actually sent to the mills. Pseudolus is the creator-slave *par excellence*. His improvisations and self-consciousness outdo even Tranio of the *Mostellaria*, and he is undoubtedly the most interesting character of the play, the one whom Plautus endows with life as well as dramatic function.

From the opening scene in which the young lover Callidorus explains his dilemma to Pseudolus, we find the typical reversal of roles characteristic of the *servus-adulescens* relationship. Callidorus asks for his orders ('equid imperas?', line 383) and Pseudolus is in command. In no other play of Plautus is the military imagery to describe the slave strategist more pervasive. Not only is Pseudolus a military strategist; he is at various moments and among other roles a cook, weaver, grave robber, Socrates, tragic villain, oracle and Greek dancer. Callidorus' father Simo calls him 'meus Ulixes' and likens his attempt to inveigle the slave girl Phoenicium from the pimp Ballio to Ulysses' theft of the statue of Pallas.[5] In the *Pseudolus*, Plautus plays with the mistaken identity plot primarily through his protagonist's role playing.

But perhaps the most interesting is his role as poet-creator to whom he compares himself in his first soliloquy:

> sed quasi poeta, tabulas quom cepit sibi,
> quaerit quod nusquam gentiumst, reperit tamen,

facit illud veri simile quod mendacium est,
nunc ego poeta fiam: viginti minas,
quae nunc nusquam sunt gentium, inveniam tamen. (lines 401–5)

> Well, after all, when a poet sits down to write, he has to start by
> looking for something which doesn't exist on this earth, and
> somehow or other he finds it; he makes a fiction look very much
> like a fact. That's what I'll do; I'll be a poet; I'll invent two
> thousand drachmas, which at present don't exist anywhere on
> earth. (p. 233)[6]

Pseudolus does finally invent twenty *minas* just as he creates
his roles, with words. All his roles and identities depend on
language. In the soliloquy quoted above, Pseudolus begins by
speaking to himself: 'tu astas solus, Pseudole' and then poses
himself a series of questions: 'quid nunc acturu's, postquam
erili filio/largitu's dictis dapsilis? ubi sunt ea?' ('That leaves
me, on my own. Now what are you going to do, eh,
Pseudolus? You've entertained your young master with a feast
of fine talk. And what does it amount to now?' p. 233). In this
soliloquy Plautus sounds as if he were speaking about his own
method of poetic creation. The twenty *minas* come to
represent not literal money, but the intrigue itself which
Pseudolus, like Plautus, invents with words.

In the following scene Pseudolus plays the oracle, replying
in Greek with the oracle's conventional response to Simo's
queries. Pseudolus boasts he will inveigle the money for
Phoenicium before the end of the day, despite his master's
being on his guard. Simo's friend Callipho, sympathetic or at
least admiring of the slave's confidence, says 'edepol mortalem
graphicum, si servat fidem!' (line 519) ('the man's a living
marvel, if he can be as good as his word', p. 237). Callipho
compares Pseudolus to a work of art; a few lines later, when
accused of collusion with Ballio, Pseudolus swears that if such
were the case,

quasi in libro quom scribuntur calamo litterae,
stilis me totum usque ulmeis conscribito.   (lines 544a–5)

> you can scribble me over from head to foot with birch rods for
> pens, like writing words in a book. (p. 238)

For Pseudolus even punishment will be like the act of writing. Self-conscious allusions to the play itself appear more frequently here than in any other Plautine comedy and serve to extend our sense of Pseudolus as surrogate artist. The first immediately precedes the slave's opening soliloquy quoted in part above. Callidorus has asked him to explain his plan; Pseudolus responds, 'nolo bis iterari, sat sic longae fiunt fabulae' (line 388) ('No point in going over it twice – plays are long enough as it is' p. 232). In his next soliloquy he speaks directly to the audience, swearing he is not simply making rash promises to amuse them:

> nam qui in scaenum provenit,
> novo modo novom aliquid inventum adferre addecet;
> si id facere nequeat, det locum illi qui queat.
>
> (lines 568–70)

> What's an actor for, if he is not to bring some new kind of
> surprise on to the stage? If he can't do that much, he'd better
> make way for someone who can. (p. 239)

It is almost as if Plautus were using his slave-creator to describe his own poetic method – a kind of improvisation.

But Pseudolus' final role is not of the stature of those he has assumed earlier in the action. After the success of his deception, he gets dead drunk. Instead of addressing himself as he had earlier in the second person, he addresses his feet. In the description he gives of himself at the party of celebration with Callidorus, he is as unselfconscious as he has been self-conscious elsewhere. Though he is still able to manipulate his master, the atmosphere of transformation has changed. Pseudolus as a Greek dancing girl is a far cry from the general, orator, tragic actor, oracle and poet he has played earlier. It is a strange ending – comic, but not without a certain pathos at the loss of such capaciousness and lifelike power.

Role-playing is not the only way Plautus explores the theme of mistaken identity in the *Pseudolus*; he also uses the more conventional mistaken identity devices of deception and disguise in the Harpax plot. Simia, whose name suggests his capacity to mimic, is to play the role of Harpax. As he tells

Pseudolus, 'numquam edepol erit ill' potior Harpax quam ego' (line 925) ('No one will make a better Harpax than I', author's trans.). Ballio's complete seduction and his reaction to the true Harpax whom he believes to be an impostor bear out this boast. The confrontation between the true Harpax and Ballio is filled with irony since the pimp believes he has caught Pseudolus in the act, whereas we know that Ballio is already victim of the very trick he thinks he is exposing. In this interchange Harpax reacts as we have seen other characters react when their identities are questioned: he accuses Ballio of madness and dreaming and appeals repeatedly to the facts of his name and rank as proof of his identity.

The *Pseudolus*, with its series of soliloquies in which the slave describes his intrigues, suggests the importance of such set speeches to characterization. Whereas realistic drama expresses the content of such speeches by a variety of techniques – gesture, stage movement, eloquent silences, directly presented action, counteraction and the like – rhetorical drama, the drama of Greece and Rome and of the Renaissance, expresses character through language. Menander and Plautus make wide use of set speeches to reveal character, to show a character recognizing his limits and failures and moving toward some greater understanding. Terence, however, except in the *Adelphoe*, rarely uses set speeches and his comedies neither portray the inner life nor parody it. Their popularity in the Renaissance as school texts and the influence of the Terentian commentaries on dramatic practice, however, require that we look at Terence in our consideration of comic characterization.

Renaissance commentators recognized the *Adelphoe* as exceptional in Terence's comic practice because Demea changes, but they also realized that his change of heart was very probably ironic. Donatus glosses line 992: 'hic ostendit Terentius magis Demeam simulasse mutatos mores quam mutavisse' ('here Terence shows Demea to pretend to changed habits rather than to be changed', author's trans.).[7] There is never any suggestion that Terence became fascinated with a character, as Plautus did with his Pseudolus, and allowed him

to escape above the chain of events in which he functioned.[8]
Characters in Terence are generally subordinated to the needs
of plot, but commentaries on Terence, because they represented a codified body of knowledge about ancient comic practice
and were used so widely in Renaissance schools, illuminate the
sixteenth-century view of comic characterization. Donatus
was undoubtedly the most important of the commentators; his
work includes two essays on comedy, the first of which we
now attribute to Evanthius, but which Renaissance scholars
believed to be his, and a line-by-line commentary on five of
Terence's six plays. The commentary went through numerous
editions and printings from the time of its rediscovery by
humanists in the fifteenth century until well into the seventeenth. Baldwin suggests that the sixteenth-century editions
alone numbered close to a thousand.

The introductory essays formed critical thinking about
comedy in the Renaissance. Toward the end of his *De Fabula*,
Evanthius provides a short summary of the differences
between tragedy and comedy which highlights the main
features of comedy as he saw them:

> inter tragoediam autem et comoediam cum multa tum imprimis
> hoc distat, quod in comoedia mediocres fortunae hominum, parvi
> impetus periculorum laetique sunt exitus actionum, at in tragoedia
> omnia contra, ingentes personae, magni timores, exitus funesti
> habentur; et illic prima turbulenta, tranquilla ultima, in tragoedia
> contrario ordine res aguntur; tum quod in tragoedia fugienda vita,
> in comoedia capessenda exprimitur; postremo quod omnis com-
> oedia de fictis est argumentis, tragoedia saepe de historia fide
> petitur.[9]

In this short paragraph we find brought together many of the
clichés about comedy which are reiterated throughout the
Renaissance and even today. Comedy deals with men of lower
fortunes, an interpretation of Aristotle's statement that
comedy deals with characters who are worse than the average.
In the sixteenth century, commentators often interpreted
Aristotle to mean that comedy deals with characters who are
guilty of minor offenses rather than grave crimes, and certainly

Evanthius' words allow for such an interpretation. We also find a brief description of comic structure – comedies begin with conflict and end in happiness and tranquility – and a rather interesting and strikingly modern phrase, that whereas in tragedy life is fled, in comedy it is seized.

Jodocus Badius Ascensius' prefatory essay to his 1502 edition of Terence's plays is the longest and most complete critical essay to accompany any of the Renaissance editions of Terence.[10] He remarks that all characters in comedy go through considerable delusion and anxiety before the happy outcome of comedy is reached; he explains that Evanthius' phrase *vitam capessendam* means comic characters reform after error. Ascensius' remark is interesting in two respects – on the one hand it suggests a perceived comic structure of change and development important to my argument; on the other it indicates what will become an increasingly important feature of Terentian commentary, its emphasis on the moral utility of his plays. Comedy teaches moral lessons, as Renaissance reformers such as Erasmus, Melanchthon and others reiterate. They draw the lessons or places which specific plays and characters represent, the examples of prudent behavior to be emulated, imprudent behavior to be avoided.

Finally Evanthius makes the old distinction, also derived from Aristotle, that comic plots are based on fiction whereas tragic plots are based on history. This claim militates against Cicero's equally influential statement that comedy is the imitation of life, a commonplace Donatus will quote in his own essay which follows. This conflict between the Ciceronian notion of comedy as an imitation of life and the Aristotelean description of the comic plot as fiction was resolved through the notion of probability or *vraisemblance*. Comedy is fictitious, but it must have a probable relation to the real. Donatus claims that this probability, which is based on recognition of the lifelike, constitutes the pleasure a reader or viewer takes in a play.

Evanthius' summary does not mention the laws of characterization so important both to the commentary itself and to Renaissance drama, but elsewhere he praises Terence's adherence to the rules of decorum, his diligence in attributing the appropriate traits to his *personae* according to their natures (*habitus*), ages (*aetas*), and fortunes (*officium*). The principle of decorum entails finding diction appropriate to the sex, rank, age, fortune and circumstances of a particular type. Evanthius attributes the dramatist's success at making the fictive arguments of comedy *fidem veritatis* to his attention to decorum in character and plotting. In his esay which follows, Donatus enumerates the types commonly found in Terentian comedy, both the major characters, the *senex, adulescens,* and *servus,* and the minor types, the *miles, leno, puella, meretrix* and *parasitus.* Terence was widely recognized for his superiority at creating characters whose language and behavior represented the types described by Aristotle and Theophrastus and passed on to Quintilian and Cicero. Terence's typical double plots required individualization within the types; the two fathers of the *Adelphoe,* for example, or the two young men of the *Andria,* were differentiated within the broad confines of their types. More importantly, Renaissance commentators recognized that in particular comic plots a character type inevitably becomes dynamic rather than static because the movement from a turbulent beginning to a tranquil end, as Evanthius puts it, or from error to reform, as Ascensius describes it, or from confusion to discovery, entails change.

Most of the work on dramatic characterization in Renaissance drama has focused on types and decorum, but by doing so, critics have been blinded to some important issues that deserve clarification.[11] We need to distinguish between decorum, which in the Renaissance represented a code for portraying various types onstage, and the actual means of rendering their speech. Speeches which manifest characteristics of dialogue such as those we have analyzed in Shakespeare's *Measure for Measure,* in Menander, and even in Plautus, create or represent an inner life regardless of how typically they may code information concerning sex, rank, fortune, or age. Instead of reciting the rules of decorum, we need to look at what Renaissance commentators have to say about the production of character.

Our judgment of a character's lifelikeness depends, as I have argued, not so much on his character traits as *how* those traits are presented through language. It may not be true, for example, that old men are avaricious and young men carried away by their desires – we may know of countless examples from life which refute such generalizations. Our perception as spectators of the lifelikeness of a character is determined not by its relation to what we know of life, but how the character is presented onstage, whether the techniques the dramatist uses make it believable. Cicero himself recognized this when he said in *De Senectute* that a person's traits depend not on his age, but on his character. Typically, he uses a literary example to prove his point: the opposing old men of the *Adelphoe*.

In *De Ratione Studii*, commonly regarded as an important shaping influence on the English grammar school, Erasmus says there are two decorums. Writers and commentators after him pick up on this distinction. One he calls *commune*, which is what we usually regard as decorum. It is general and requires that a character conform to the commonly recognized characteristics of his age, class, fortune, sex. But there was also what Erasmus called *peculiare*, or individual decorum. He, like Cicero, takes Terence as his example, arguing that the dramatist individualizes pairs of all three major types – old men, young lovers, slaves. In the *De Copia Rerum* he remarks that comic poets especially seem to have striven for variety in creating characters of the same type. Erasmus also noted that this pairing was not simply a function of Terentian double plots because Terence also distinguishes among type characters from play to play. The notion of individuation, of creating individualized characters, is not as foreign to the Renaissance as the emphasis given to decorum by modern critics makes it seem.[12]

Renaissance commentators and rhetoricians generally agree that impersonation is the most effective technique for creating character regardless of what name they give the figure. In our discussion of Menander it is called *prosopopoeia*, as it was by Aphthonius and Quintilian (IX, ii, 29–32), but Willichius, for example, called it *dialogismos*, while Donatus named it *mimesis*. All three terms, however, are illustrated with similar examples in which the author or a character impersonates the words of another character or person through an imaginary dialogue. A commonly cited example from the *Adelphoe* is Micio's impersonation of his brother in the plays opening monologue. There we learn that Demea and Micio have opposite notions of child-rearing, one strict and even harshly austere, the other overly kind, even indulgent. Micio distinguishes between *pater* and *dominus*, claiming he is a father rather than a master to his son. The brothers, as Renaissance commentators recognized, are individualized representatives of a common type, the *senex*. To emphasize the contrast between them, Terence uses a conventional country/city dichotomy: Demea lives in the country, which represents thrift, sound values and hard work; Micio in the city, which typifies licentiousness and luxury.

Terence distinguishes between the two throughout the play: at I, ii, for example, Micio says to his brother, 'natura tu illi pater es, consiliis ego' (line 126) (You're his father by blood; I'm his father at heart).[13] *Consilium* here means 'understanding,' though Copley translates it as 'heart.' Micio and Aeschinus are not bound by nature, since Aeschinus is actually Demea's son whom Micio has raised, but by a shared understanding and sense of purpose. But when Demea leaves the scene, we learn that Micio is more upset than he has let on; with his brother he has assumed a casual unconcern, but the latest of Aeschinus' escapades has begun to shake even his firm faith.

In the last act, Demea assumes Micio's fatherly role, forcing his brother to recognize the limitations of his method of child-rearing. Demea has pleaded throughout the action that Micio be as strict with Aeschinus as he is with Ctesipho; when Micio will not comply, Demea self-consciously assumes his brother's identity and thereby pushes Micio into his: 'nunc tu germanu's pariter animo et corpore' (line 957) (Now you really are my brother, body and soul, p. 165). Terence represents both characters as learning that they must balance an understanding of the humanness of their sons' behavior with a sense of parental responsibility and authority. Hegio, friend to both fathers and common moral denominator for both, tells us the young men's actions are only human (pp. 470–1).

The didactic function of the *Adelphoe* and of Terentian comedy generally made Terence a favourite of Renaissance scholars whose commentaries become increasingly moral and didactic in the course of the sixteenth century. Whereas Donatus glosses primarily explain usage, quote from other Latin and Greek authors, and explicate particular words or meanings, Renaissance commentators increasingly use the plays to illustrate moral lessons, most certainly a habit which derives from Erasmus. The distance between the plays themselves and the moral lessons they are said to demonstrate grows steadily. An excellent example is the handling of Terence's treatment of the courtesan. Evanthius, who praises Terence's success at creating characters who conform to their types, points out that his courtesans, as in the *Andria*, instead of being immoral, avaricious and vulgar, are sometimes virtuous. He hastens to add that the dramatist is always careful to motivate such divergences from the type. Renaissance commentators repeat this exception, but not always with Evanthius' perspicuity. As the fervor to use plays for demonstrating moral lessons grows, commentators such as Willichius dispute this sympathetic portrayal by assuring their readers that the courtesan's positive character is artful; hers is only a seeming virtue.[14] In other words, the generic conventions for the rendering of types, which after all conform to socially coded rules or perceptions of behavior shaped in this period by the moral climate of the Reformation, obscure the actual presentation of character in Terence's plays.

Whereas Menander seeks to portray an individual's learning process within the structural conventions of the comic plot, and Plautus uses such themes primarily for comedy, Terence is preoccupied with dramatizing familial and social relationships. In the *Hecyra* for example, instead of the individual's ethical and moral journey toward self-knowledge, Terence dramatizes familial relationships, filial duty and loyalty. In that play, the mistakes the fathers make about their wives show Terence altering conventions of characterization. The *matrona* in the *Hecyra* is not at fault through her meddling or dislike of her young daughter-in-law, just as Bacchis, despite the opening scene's unfavorable portrayal of courtesans, turns out to be moral and virtuous. Finally the slave in this play is not responsible for the deception or the discovery.

Though Terence does not endow the Adelphoe themselves with the rhetoric of consciousness we find in Menander and Plautus, his use of the double plot and juxtaposition of the brothers' two opposing points of view creates a dialogue which serves to individualize his characters. As audience we come to know each brother and to have a sense of both as individuals despite their conventional types and attitudes. Baldwin and others have argued persuasively for the influence of Terentian double plots on Shakespeare's dramatic structure; though Terence does not attempt to create an inner life for his characters through soliloquy and the rhetoric of consciousness, his plays and their commentaries demonstrated to the Renaissance playwright how he might individualize his *personae* within the confines of their types by juxtaposing two examples of the same type endowed with distinctive characteristics. His double plots and type characters are not simply a mechanical innovation, but a technique which has profound effect on meaning and interpretation in Renaissance drama. In sixteenth-century comedy such doubling, as in *As You Like It*, makes for psychological complexity and what we call lifelikeness even without the rhetoric of consciousness we find in Menander, in Plautus, and later in Shakespeare.

The general revival of classical studies and the fifteenth-century manuscript discoveries contributed to the dramatic revival of the Italian Renaissance. Italian drama influenced by Plautus and Terence falls into three categories: comedies in Latin modeled at least in part on ancient plays; performances of Plautus and Terence onstage; and most important, vernacular Italian comedies or *commedie erudite* based on Latin models. The English playwrights derived their dramatic models in part directly from Roman drama, but also in part from continental European drama, especially the Italian. In order, therefore, to understand the uses to which Shakespeare puts the conventions of mistaken identity and the rhetoric of the inner life he inherits from the ancients, we must examine representative Italian plays which illustrate and develop such rhetoric and conventions.

5

The enchantments of Circe

These be the enchantments of Circe brought out of Italy to mar men's manners in England: much by example of ill life but more by precepts of fond books, of late translated out of Italian into English, sold in every shop in London, commended by honest titles the sooner to corrupt honest manners; dedicated over-boldly to virtuous and honourable personages, the easier to beguile simple and innocent wits.

(Ascham, *The Scholemaster*, 1570)

The major works of the Italian Renaissance – those of Petrarch, Ariosto, Castiglione and Tasso – were widely printed, translated and read in Elizabethan England. The Italian literary example inspired not only the English love lyric and the epic, but also the short story, civil treatise and romance. The English popular theatre ransacked the Italian *novelle* for plots, but the evidence of Italian plays printed, performed or directly imitated is scarce indeed.[1] Records of the Office of Revels do refer to performances by Italian companies at court and the Acts of the Privy Council record payments made to these traveling players. In 1573, for example, we know that an Italian company not only performed at court, but stayed on a year acting in other parts of England along the royal progress.[2] There are also, of course, a few early imitations of specific Italian plays such as Gascoigne's *Supposes* (1566), based on Ariosto's *I Suppositi*; Jeffere's *The Bugbears* (1565), based mainly on Grazzini's *La Spiritata*; and an English *Fedele and Fortunio: Two Gentlemen* (1585), a version of Pasqualigo's *Il Fedele*. As early as the 1540s there is evidence of the performance of a play based on Charles Estienne's *Le Sacrifice* (1543), later *Les Abusez*, a translation of *Gl'Ingannati*, which may or may not be related to the Latin verse *Laelia* acted at Queen's College, Cambridge, in 1595.

To judge that Italian comedy did not influence Elizabethan drama from such meagre statistics is to ignore the testimony of other kinds of historical and generic evidence.[3] Anti-theatrical tracts provide revealing corroborative evidence of the knowledge of Italian Renaissance comedy in Elizabethan England. Italy was so readily identified with comedy that in his *Plays Confuted in Five Actions* (1582), Stephen Gosson uses the terms 'comedies' and 'Italian devises' almost interchangeably. 'Baudie comedies', he complains, are corrupting the London stage because whoever cannot read 'Italian bawdry' is presented with 'comedies cut from the same pattern'.

In *The Schoole of Abuse* (1579), despite its anti-Italian sentiment, he notes that the Italians made certain improvements on classical comedies. Gosson realized that Italian playwrights altered the conventions of plot and character inherited from Latin comedy:

> The lewdenes of Gods, is altered and chaunged to the love of young men: force, to friendshippe; rapes to mariage; woing allowed by assurance of wedding, privie meetings of bahcelours [*sic*] and maidens on the stage, not as murderers that devour the good name ech of other in their mindes, but as those that desire to bee made one in hearte.[4]

Gosson's remarks suggest that he recognized some of the technical and thematic innovations made by Italian dramatists.

Until very recently, Gosson's insight has gone unnoted; Italian comedy has long been considered essentially derivative, a version of Latin intrigue unworthy of serious reading and interpretation.[5]

In the last fifteen years, however, critics have begun to study generic and textual relationships between late Italian Renaissance drama and Shakespeare's problem comedies and romances. G. K. Hunter has pointed out specific verbal parallels between *All's Well that Ends Well* and *Il Pastor Fido*.[6] The providential structure of the later comedies has been linked to Italian pastoral tragicomedy, specifically to *Il Pastor Fido* and *Aminta*, which were enormously popular and often printed between 1591 and Shakespeare's death.[7] Louise George Clubb relates Shakespeare's Helena and Isabella, and the heroines of the later romances, to a generic figure of late Italian comedy whom she describes as the woman as wonder, a type clearly distinguishable from the enterprising *innamorata* of earlier Italian plays.[8]

If we turn to Shakespeare's romantic comedy, however, the question of Italian influence remains problematic. Despite Clubb's evidence that the *commedia grave*, so-called for its moral and aesthetic seriousness, contributed 'increased emotional tensions, the fuller characterization and articulateness of the lovers ... and the sad or sinister direction of the action to Shakespeare's comic practice from *The Comedy of Errors* through *Measure for Measure*', critics persist in old prejudices about Shakespeare's genius in creating romantic comedy.[9] Though Shakespeare is no longer credited with inventing a new genre, romantic comedy, Shakespeareans do continue to claim that he contributed emotional depth and interest to what was merely intrigue comedy and complicated farce. Even so astute a reader as Leo Salingar speaks in his recent book, *Shakespeare and the Traditions of Comedy*, of a

> fundamental innovation which in its general effect distinguishes Shakespeare's plays from all previous comedies, that he gives his people the quality of an inner life. Their inner life, with their capacity for introspection, changes the whole bearing of the incidents that make up a traditional comic plot.[10]

But if we look at *Gl'Ingannati* (1531), a play by the Sienese academy, the Intronati, which is much alluded to but seldom carefully read, we find that many of the features traditionally attributed to Shakespeare's achievement in romantic comedy are already present in this early Italian play commonly considered an analogue to *Twelfth Night*. A comparison often made between *Twelfth Night* and *Gl'Ingannati* illustrates the critical commonplace said to distinguish Shakespearean romantic comedy from Italian 'intrigue' comedy. Before the action of *Gl'Ingannati* begins, Lelia, the Viola figure, is in love with Flamminio (Orsino), but he has deserted her for Isabella. Lelia dons her disguise deliberately to reclaim Flamminio's love. Though Salingar calls her 'the first seriously romantic heroine on the Renaissance stage', he also claims that by making Viola fall in love with Orsino after she is disguised rather than before, Shakespeare emphasizes the romantic rather than the intrigue plot.[11] Our attention is shifted 'from the circumstances of the love story to the sentiments as such'.[12] But a careful look at *Gl'Ingannati* suggests that, as in *Twelfth Night*, the sentiments engage our attention and sympathy more than the circumstances of the love story.

Like Rosalind's disguise in *As You Like It* and Viola's in *Twelfth Night*, Lelia's is from the outset a dramatic strategy to give her freedom of speech and action not otherwise permitted an *innamorata*.[13] In the self-conscious exposition in I, iii, she describes for her nurse her reactions to Flamminio's past professions of love, reactions so guarded and innocent that the disguise seems necessary to free her true emotions and allow her to act on behalf of her love. Renaissance readers and theatergoers recognized this psychological function of masking. At the end of a spirited attack on carnival masking no doubt prompted by Castiglione's discussion of masquerade in *Il Cortegiano*, Tommaso Garzoni suggests that disguise has four notable effects: 'it makes one bold, because his person is not known, it hides the poverty of those who are badly dressed, it teaches the shamefaced to speak, and it gives freedom to personages of gravity and respect'.[14] The disguise

convention is the dramatic instrument for exploring complex-
ities of personality – the limitations of self-definition and
sexual roles and the desire to present the self in ways which
liberate rather than limit action – all within the safe confines of
a disguise or role.

Flamminio's fickleness and hopeless professions of passion,
like Orsino's in *Twelfth Night*, are a pose, a role he plays,
however unconsciously, to avoid committing himself to love.
Lelia early in the play tells us that Flamminio had shown a
marked affection for a young page recently dead; it is this
knowledge that prompts her to disguise herself as a boy to win
his love. He can love her only when she is dressed as a boy
because such love requires none of the institutional and
emotional commitments of adult sexuality and marriage. In
their first interview in II, i, Lelia in disguise begins to win back
her beloved by helping him to see his past behavior in a new
way. When he wonders why Isabella refuses his letters and
embassies and claims in an extravagant courtly pledge that he
will follow her to death, Lelia asks if there is not some lady
equal in virtue and beauty to Isabella who would love him.
Love, she asserts, should be reciprocal. When he tells of his
former love for Lelia, she contends that Isabella's disdain is
punishment for his sin in leaving his first love:

> Il qual peccato non so se Iddio ve lo possa mai perdonare. Ahi,
> signor Flamminio! Voi fate per certo un gran male.[15]

> That's a sin, and I don't know whether God can ever pardon it.
> O, Signor Flamminio! You're certainly doing something
> very wrong.[16]

Flamminio's response is ironic: 'Tu sei ancora un putto, Fabio,
e non puoi cognoscere la forza d'amore' (p. 151) ('You're still a
child [boy], Fabio, and you can't be expected to understand
the full force of love', p. 216). Both Flamminio and later
Orsino believe they are men who understand the force of love
better than the boys who serve them, but we in the audience
know differently.

In their next interview when Lelia reports Isabella's refusal, it is Flamminio who connects Isabella's disdain with his former love for Lelia. He fears she may believe he still loves Lelia and he is determined to make her understand otherwise:

> Ma io gli farò intendere ch'io non l'amo più; anzi l'ho in odio e non la posso sentir ricordare. (p. 167)

> But I'll show her that I don't love Lelia any more – that I hate her in fact, and can't even bear to hear her name mentioned. (p. 228)

Despite his harsh rejection of Lelia, so fraught with irony to the knowing audience, Flamminio has begun to change. He now recognizes a causal relationship between his past love and present distress, though as yet he cannot admit his fault. Overcome by Flamminio's scorn, Lelia/Fabio faints. Flamminio's reaction is another step toward his crucial recognition at the end of the play. Here he begins to value reciprocity in love:

> ch'io non so se fusse mai al mondo servidor più accorto, meglio accostumato di questo giovanetto; ed, oltre a questo, mostra d'amarmi tanto che, se fusse donna, pensarei che la stesse mal di me. (p. 167)

> I don't think there's ever been a cleverer, better-mannered servant anywhere than this one. And what's more, he seems so attached to me that if he were a woman I'd think he was ill for love of me. (p. 228)

These two scenes dramatize Flamminio's growing realization that he has failed to follow the courtly code he so fervently professes.

At the end of this interview, the Italian authors use the comic soliloquy to present Lelia's feelings and internal conflict excited by Flamminio's repudiation. Her soliloquy, like Angelo's in *Measure for Measure* and the examples we have considered from classical comedy, is marked by the linguistic features of dialogue. The Intronati seek to represent a mind in conflict with itself:

Or hai pur, misera te, con le tue propie [sic] orecchie,
dall'istessa bocca di questo ingrato di Flamminio, inteso
quanto egli t'ami, misera, scontenta Lelia! Perché più
perdi tempo in servir questo crudele? Non ti è giovata la
pazienzia, non i preghi, non i favori che gli hai fatti; or non
ti giovan gl'inganni. Sventurata me! Rifiutata, scacciata,
fuggita, odiata! Perché servi'io a chi mi rifiuta? Perché
domando chi mi scaccia? Perché seguo chi mi fugge?
Perché amo chi m'ha in odio. Ah! Flamminio. Non ti piace
se non Isabella. Egli non vuole altro che Isabella. Abbisela,
tenghisela; ch'io lo lascierò o morrò. Delibero di non
più servirli in questo abito né più capitargli innanzi,
poiché tanto m'ha in odio. Andarò a trovar Clemenzia,
che so che m'aspetta in casa, e con essa disporrò quel che
abbi da essere della vita mia. (p. 168)

Well, now you've heard it all with your own ears, from
Flamminio's ungrateful lips – you've heard just how much
he loves you! Poor, unfortunate Lelia! Why waste any
more time in the service of this cruel man? [The second
person is suppressed in the English translation] You
achieved nothing with your patience, your prayers, or the
kindness you showed him earlier on; and now you've
achieved nothing by deceit. Poor, poor Lelia! Rejected,
driven away, shunned and hated! Why should I serve a man
who rejects me, why seek a man who drives me away, why
follow a man who shuns me, why love a man who hates me?
Oh Flamminio! nothing pleases you except Isabella! You
don't want anything but Isabella! Very well then – win her,
keep her if you will. I'll leave you or die in the attempt – I
won't serve him anymore, or wear these clothes, or even see
him again, since he hates me so much. I'll go and find
Clemenzia, who's waiting for me in her house, I know, and
with her help I'll decide what to do with my life.
(pp. 228–9)

Here we find the pronominal contrasts of 'I' and 'you' in the
first and second person verb forms and pronouns remarked in
earlier soliloquies. The second person rhetorical question,
'Perché più perdi tempo in servir questo crudele?' is juxtaposed
to the first person 'Perché serv'io a chi mi rifiuta?' The
repeated rhetorical questions here and throughout the soliloquy serve both to represent Lelia in a dialogue with herself and

to compel us to sympathize with her plight. Just as in Angelo's soliloquy, the shift back and forth between first and second person and the apostrophe, 'misera te', serve to enhance the expressive or emotive function of the speech. As in *Measure for Measure*, we find the semantic reversals characteristic of dialogue. The often hyperbolic antitheses, *servire/rifiutare; domandare/scacciare; seguire/fuggire; amare/aver in odio* represent the two poles of conflict in Lelia's mind. The string of past participles and the alternating rhetorical questions, each of which repeats the preceding verb in another form, provide an ordered framework which moves the audience toward the emotional climax of Lelia's apostrophe, 'Ah, Flamminio.' Other features of dialogue are the temporal markers and verb tenses which locate this speech in the specific situation and the series of past participles describing Flamminio's treatment of Lelia which alternate with the present tenses describing her action now. This soliloquy, generated by Flamminio's denial of her identity as his beloved, manifests the now familiar rhetoric of consciousness or inner debate.

Though the soliloquies of Lelia and Angelo share many features, they serve quite different functions in their respective plots. Angelo's speech, which comes early in the action before the conflict is fully established, presents his response to a surprising discovery about himself; Lelia's comes at the last possible moment before the *anagnorisis* which resolves the complicated intrigue. Its function is to present an emotional climax and to increase suspense by having the *innamorata* decide to give up her seemingly hopeless suit. Instead of the series of analogies which move us from one idea to the next in Angelo's soliloquy and reveal a mind rooted in the concrete realities of nature and society, the Italian playwrights use repetition to build an emotional climax in which we see a disconsolate Lelia decide on a new course of action. The simple, repeated syntactic forms – the 'non' clauses (lines 5–7), the series of participles (lines 8–9), and the questions beginning 'perché' (lines 10–12) – are balanced by a corresponding semantic richness.[17] The carefully graduated 'pazienza, preghi, favori', and the series of similarly progressive participles, which are repeated in the following rhetorical questions, move the audience by steps toward the climactic apostrophe to Flamminio.

Like Viola in her soliloquy in II, ii, 16 ff., Lelia repudiates not only her disguise, but deception itself: 'non ti giovan gl'inganni'. Her disguise tests her love as well as Flamminio's by subjecting it to his harsh rejection. Unlike Viola, however, Lelia trusts not in time, but in her nurse Clemenzia to help her resolve her predicament. But if we look at the scene in which Clemenzia confronts Flamminio, again we find his feelings rather than the intrigue to be the focus of the action. When Flamminio discovers that Isabella loves Fabio, his jealousy, like Orsino's, is uncontrollable. The nurse takes over Lelia's role as teacher/confessor and leads Flamminio by means of a fable, a disguised description of his own story, to condemn his own behavior and admit Lelia's devotion: 'Beato lui! Felice lui! Questo non potrò già dir io. ... Io dico che costui non può esser cavaliere, anzi è un traditore', (p. 221) ('Lucky man! Lucky, lucky man! I'll never be the hero of a story like that! ... He can't be a knight! He's a traitor', p. 271).[18] Flamminio's ignorance is pitted against Clemenzia's manipulative knowledge: the irony which results is instructive and purgative, for not only does it teach him at last the behavior of a true *cavaliere*, but it also serves to expiate his sins.

When he learns Fabio's true identity, he admits his guilt and repents of his errors saying, 'E perdonatemi se qualche dispiacere v'ho io fatto, non cognoscendovi; perch'io ne son pentitissimo e accorgomi dell'error mio' (p. 225) ('Forgive me for the pain I gave you when I didn't know who you were – I repent of that most heartily and admit that I was in the wrong', p. 274).[19] The verb *conoscere* is used six times in this short scene along with verbs having similar meanings (seeing, believing, understanding, marveling), always with the adverb *bene*, for Flamminio is finally able to know himself and Lelia. Though the characters are deceived about the other characters, more importantly they are deceived about themselves. Isabella's love for Fabio, like Olivia's for Cesario, is represented within the action of the play as a narcissistic love of self which the references to the effeminacy of the pages continually emphasize.

Gl'Ingannati is unlike earlier comedies based on disguise and intrigue in its emphasis on feeling and the internal development of its characters.[20] This emphasis on sentiment prefigures later developments in Italian comedy, but we may account for it more directly by looking at the place and circumstances of the play's composition. *Gl'Ingannati* was written anonymously by members of the Sienese academy known as the Intronati, a group of educated humanists and aristocrats who attempted, with a healthy dose of ironic distance, to live out Castiglione's prescriptions in *Il Corte-giano* that the perfect courtier should make even his quotidian activities examples of perfection. According to the prologue, the play was written in three days to compensate for an allegorical spectacle presented on Epiphany called *Il Sacrificio* in which members of the academy sacrificed remembrances of their ladies to Minerva in hopes of freeing themselves from the bonds of love.[21] The prologue is spoken by an actor sent as ambassador to reclaim the friendship of the noble ladies offended by the misogyny of *Il Sacrificio*. Filled as it is with double entendre, the prologue presents itself and the play to follow almost as a means of seduction, a graceful, courtly and at the same time lascivious way of winning the love of the ladies in the audience. At its end, the speaker presents a moral to be gleaned from attending the play: love is worth the patience coupled with good conduct that it demands.

Recent work on the relationship between Italian Renaissance society and dramatic production suggests that the pronounced preference for comedy not only in Siena, but in Florence, Ferrara and Venice as well, testifies to an aristocratic public, spectators for whom the entertainment and bawdy joking of comedy were an extension and product of a hedonistic, indulgent courtly class which produced as well as consumed its own theatricals.[22] The educated humanists, often nobility themselves, wrote for the court at Ferrara or for the powerful urban ruling families of Florence and Tuscany. Tragedy, concerned as it is with the actions of superior persons in relation to power, offered unwanted commentary on the social and political organization of the Italian city states; comedy, with its characters from the wealthy mercantile class, was less dangerous and therefore flourished in the humanist productions which were written and produced for the festive spectacles designed to demonstrate and consolidate the power of the ruling classes. Castelvetro commented cynically that New Comedy was fostered by monarchs and aristocrats 'because it does not rebuke any of their operations, ... or stir up the common people'.[23] Such an interpretation of the social and political forces of Italian Renaissance culture accounts in part for the extraordinary proliferation of comedy and its sometimes startling repetition of plots and character types, but we need to consider as well the prologue and circumstances of *Gl'Ingannati's* writing and production.

These plays were also part of a complex rhetoric and structure of courtly behavior. They were written and produced for audiences preoccupied with relations between the sexes – the Intronati's plays were avowedly amorous, presented to an audience of 'nobilissime donne'. Many of the comedies were written and performed as part of the festive occasions which marked the marriages of members of the ruling classes. Over and over again the plays are concerned not simply with the means of love, with dramatizing the Boccaccian strategies and intrigues which win sexual pleasure, but also with the psychology of love, with courtship, with vows of fidelity, and responses to the vicissitudes of fortune in relation to the constancy of love. The many examples of constancy and enterprise in winning love which the plays represent were designed to affect the audiences for which they were written, both to tickle their taste for pleasurable entertainment and to represent models of courtly behavior and its luscious fruits. The emphasis on feeling and development of character in *Gl'Ingannati* and plays like it is a dramatization of courtly modes of action and psychology worked out within the inherited conventions of the comic stage. The plays dramatized not simply literary codes inherited from Boccaccio and Ariosto, but codes of behavior which the spectators imagined themselves, with some irony, to be living. Sentiment, psychology, change were presented through the conventional language of dramatic comedy; *Gl'Ingannati*, written with boasted courtly *sprezzatura* in only three days, dramatized these sentiments without excluding the sensual, lascivious joking of intrigue.

Gl'Ingannati does not present characters equal in depth and interest to those of Shakespeare's mature comedies, but it does provide a model for the way in which the Italian dramatists linked mistaken identity plots with themes of forgiveness and self-knowledge to represent character development. Shakespeare and the Intronati use the comic soliloquy with its characteristic features of dialogue – rhetorical questions, self-address, a peculiar use of pronouns, paradox – to dramatize the feelings and inner lives of their protagonists. Missing from *Gl'Ingannati*, as Salingar points out, are the 'more mysterious and irrational aspects' of love, that sense of wonder so important to *Twelfth Night*.[24] To Shakespeare's Sebastian, the world of Illyria seems strange and fantastic; he believes he is 'mad, or else this is a dream'. Like so many of Shakespeare's characters, Sebastian must lose himself to find himself. He realizes, however, that in his free act of marrying Olivia:

> though 'tis wonder that enwraps me thus,
> Yet 'tis not madness

Madness and self-knowledge are represented in *Gl'Ingannati* by the names of the opposing inns in which Fabrizio, the Sebastian figure, is invited to stay. The hosts debate the merits of their respective establishments, the Specchio (mirror) and the Matto (madman). As the pedant points out to anyone willing to listen, the mirror signifies wisdom according to Cato's maxim, *nosce teipsum*, know thyself, (III, ii). But the play lacks any mediating sense of wonder which partakes of both the rational and the supra-rational, the mirror and the madman.

The wonder so important to Shakespeare's late comedies and final romances, though missing from *Gl'Ingannati*, is found in later Italian comedy in the so-called *commedia grave*.[25] In the antepenultimate scene of *Gl'Ingannati*, we find the language of sin and forgiveness so important to Shakespeare's later comedies, but here such language is primarily metaphorical, a way of expressing the rigors of love rather than an attempt to endow love with serious religious significance. In the later Italian *commedie gravi* influenced by the sentiments and politics of the Counter-Reformation and often based on *novelle* derived from romance, the potential for serious or near-tragic action is greater than the jealous threats of Flamminio; the power of the hero's recognition of guilt and movement toward self-knowledge is correspondingly more significant.

In many of these plays, extraordinary constancy in love excites both the audience and the characters of the play to wonder. Piccolomini's *Amor Costante*, Borghini's *La Donna Costante* and Sforza Oddi's *L'Erophilomachia*, though they vary in the particulars of their plots, are all designed to provide examples of constancy in love. In each play, two lovers, separated by fortune and subjected to a series of disasters, from pirates and slavery to family feuds, withstand all the trials of fortune and maintain their love. In such a plot, it is easy to see how a change in character is unimportant, even contrary, to the purposes of a playwright whose aim is to portray constancy rather than development or change. The various disguises in these plays, instead of motivating moments of internal confusion, cause external complications or play with quasi-religious themes.

This kind of static characterization is neither simply a feature of the theme of constant love nor a result of conservative views of female duty and character, because in Oddi's play, the most passive and self-sacrificing role is played by the male protagonist, Leandro; it also represents a religious and political perspective common in much post-Tridentine comedy which tends to praise passivity and perseverance as virtues sanctioned by Counter-Reformation forces in church and government.[26] But not all of the later plays represent characters as passive and unchanging, in a fixed order overseen by providence. Consider, for example, Bargagli's *La*

Pellegrina, one of the finest of the later Italian serious comedies, deserving of close attention in its own right. The play, first published in 1589, was written for the royal wedding of Ferdinand de' Medici and Christine of Lorraine more than twenty years earlier. John Florio lists it as one of his sources for *A Worlde of Wordes* (1598), which suggests that it was in England prior to that date. The pilgrim Drusilla resembles Helena in *All's Well* in her unfaltering devotion to Lucrezio; he is subject to vicissitude and error for which he must confess, repent and be forgiven.[27] His development and movement toward self-knowledge are linked directly with ritual confession and repentance within a disguise plot entailing Drusilla's miraculous rebirth.

While in Spain Lucrezio falls in love with the virtuous Drusilla; required to go back to Italy, he vows to return in one year.[28] Lucrezio breaks his promise and a friend who has been to Valencia tells him of the death of his beloved and describes seeing her on a funeral bier. Though this detail exculpates Lucrezio's desertion to some degree, he is not guiltless. When the play opens, he has promised his relations he will marry Lepida. Meanwhile she feigns madness to avoid the marriage because of her love for Terenzio. Drusilla, having awakened from what was only a deathlike swoon, makes a religious pilgrimage from Spain in disguise to seek her lover. After many intrigues and confusions in which Drusilla is benefactress and conscience to the other characters, the two lovers are at last reunited. The final scenes are particularly significant for the portrayal of feeling and sentiment and the relationship of the mistaken identity plot to character development in the *commedia grave*.

Unlike Flamminio in *Gl'Ingannati*, Lucrezio recognizes from the outset that he has sinned in not returning to Spain. In I, iv, he tells his confidante, 'io ho un grave peccato addosso che mi rode l'animo di continuo' ('I am to blame for a grievous sin which gnaws at my soul continually', author's trans.).[29] He goes on to explain how he fell in love with Drusilla, to stress her virtue in refusing his advances, even his kiss, until they could be publicly as well as privately plighted. In this way

Drusilla's virtue is carefully emphasized and she is distinguished from Lepida, the other *innamorata* who has made a
similar vow to Terenzio and who is now pregnant.[30] Lucrezio,
whose name resounds both with pagan associations to the
virtuous Lucretia and with contemporary references to
Machiavelli's Lucrezia, reports that bankruptcy and financial
disasters prevented him from returning to Spain at the
appointed time. Now he is overcome with grief at his friend's
report of Drusilla's death. Lucrezio's servant Carletto believes
his master's distress to be caused by a mercantile loss, but
Lucrezio claims:

> Dio l'avesse voluto! Ché perdita di robba non mi arebbe potuto
> tenere due giorni in simil dolore.
>
> (I, iv, 144–5)

> That God had willed it so! For the loss of goods would not have
> made me this sad even two days. (author's trans.)

Nevertheless, we know from Lucrezio's preceding explanation to Carletto that such losses did prevent him from keeping
his promise to Drusilla. Lucrezio fails his beloved in order to
preserve his material wealth.

We need to look closely at what this detail of the plot
signifies in the play and within the larger context of Italian
comedy. Comic plots were traditionally based on a fundamental binomial, eros and money.[31] These two elements combine
in a seemingly infinite number of permutations to generate
comic plots. They are also reciprocal because in both classical
and early Italian comedy, money is required to gain love –
whether simply as payment for the courtesans and prostitutes
of classical and early Italian comedy, or as the price of winning
the *innamorata* in marriage. The importance of this dichotomy
is as clear in Shakespeare as in Italian comedy – in *The
Merchant of Venice*, *Much Ado*, and *Measure for Measure*. In
post-Tridentine Italian comedy, however, in which constancy
and the sentiments of the lovers have become the subject of the
action, this reciprocal relation between money and eros is
called into question. So in *La Pellegrina*, Lucrezio's efforts to
recoup his financial losses lead him to the 'sin' of deserting

Drusilla. In the traditional comic plot the love impulse is first opposed to the social order because it motivates the lover and his confidante to a series of anti-social actions on behalf of his beloved. These actions often involve the quest for money or its dishonest use for bribes and the like, but the anti-social impulse is almost always recuperated by the reintegration of the lover and his beloved through marriage into the social order at the end of the play. In *La Pellegrina*, however, Lucrezio's attention to money leads to the loss rather than the gain of his love.

Despite Lucrezio's failure to return and his weakness in allowing his relations to persuade him to marry Lepida, we learn in his first interview with the disguised Drusilla of his unwillingness to go through with the marriage. Having heard of the pilgrim's reputation as a healer, he asks her to see his betrothed and determine the nature of her illness. When Drusilla asks him if he will go ahead with the marriage when he knows Lepida to be well, he says he doesn't want to. When she asks why he wants her to see Lepida at all, he says he wants Lepida's madness verified so that he can excuse himself to his father from marriage to her. What is interesting about this scene, however, is the careful way in which Bargagli emphasizes Lucrezio's inability to recognize his beloved. She herself reflects on whether she has changed so much, whether her disguise has so transfigured her, that Lucrezio is unable to recognize her. Most important, however, is her speculation on how he has changed:

> Oh Dio, com'è possibile ch'io sia tanto mutata da quel di prima o che questo abito mi trasfiguri tanto che Lucrezio non m'abbia conosciuta? Anzi, mutato sei tu, Lucrezio, e hai rivolto di maniera l'animo altrove che non riconosci più Drusilla tua. É possibile che né il volto né gli atti né le parole non te n'abbiano fatto sovvenire.
>
> (II, vii, 133–8)

> Oh God, how is it possible that I could be so changed from what I was, or that this habit transforms me, that Lucrezio should not recognize me? No, you are changed, Lucrezio, and your heart has turned elsewhere so that you no longer know your Drusilla. Is it possible that neither my face, nor my gestures, nor my words have made you remember? (author's trans.)

Her disguise as a pilgrim and his inability to recognize her proceed from his 'revolt' from loving her. His failure to remain constant to his love, though mitigated by circumstances, is nevertheless an obstacle which prevents him from recognizing his beloved. Drusilla's disguise is a literal extension of the change which led him, however unwillingly, to forsake her.

The lover's reconciliation follows the union of Lepida and Terenzio which releases Lucrezio from any commitment to Lepida. In response to Lucrezio's thanks for her help in freeing him from Lepida, Drusilla tells him that his suffering was the result of a sin from which he will never be free until he repents and atones. Lucrezio was 'deceived' by Lepida because he has deceived some other woman. When he protests that though he has many faults, this is one he has never committed, Drusilla responds by telling him she knows of his promises to someone else in Valencia. Still Lucrezio cannot recognize her, for he protests his innocence, saying that he knows his beloved to be dead. Drusilla chastises him for not returning to Spain and finding out for sure whether or not his beloved lives. Finally the pilgrim tells him Drusilla lives, but Lucrezio misunderstands, saying he knows she lives in heaven. Assured at last of his continuing love, she reveals herself. At last he can recognize her, purified by confession, repentance and atonement:

> *Pellegrina.* E me riconoscete or voi?
> *Lucrezio.* Ohimè, sète voi Drusilla? Drusilla morta o pur
> risuscitata? Che cosa è questa?
> *Pellegrina.* Non temete, Lucrezio mio. Io son la vostra Drusilla
> viva e non morta e non morii mai. Né fu però bugiardo
> quel vostra amico, perch'io fui tenuta per morta molt'ore per
> un grave accidente, che saprete poi, e fin posta nella bara,
> dove egli mi vide.
> *Lucrezio.* Oh Drusilla! Io pur vi riconosco. Drusilla mia dolce,
> Drusilla mia divina, dunque non eravate voi morta?
> *Pellegrina.* Io era morta, essendo priva di voi che sète la mia
> vita, e ora risuscito, ché, racquistando voi, racquisto
> insieme lo spirito.
>
> (V, vi, 169–80)

Pellegrina. Now do you recognize me?
Lucrezio. Oh me, are you Drusilla? Drusilla dead or returned to
life? What are you?
Drusilla. Do not fear, my Lucrezio. I am your Drusilla, living
and not dead, never dead at all. Your friend was wrong, for I
was believed dead for many hours through a serious accident,
which I will tell you of later, and placed on a bier where your
friend saw me.
Lucrezio. Oh Drusilla! I recognize you. Drusilla my sweet,
divine Drusilla, then you were never dead?
Drusilla. I was dead, being deprived of you who are my life, and
now I am alive again, for having recovered you, I have
recovered my soul.

(author's trans.)

Drusilla's pilgrimage for love which ends in her reconciliation
with Lucrezio is linked with the Christian themes of
forgiveness and miraculous resurrection and offers a theatrical
image integrating the secular and the religious. The pilgrimage
itself is a metaphor for the journey toward self-understanding
which Drusilla helps Lucrezio make, just as being thought
married to the madwoman Lepida represents the suffering
necessary before he can obtain Drusilla's love. The pilgrimage
in the play – like Helena's in *All's Well* or the journey to the
wood outside Athens, the forest of Arden or the pastoral
festival of Bohemia – though here more self-consciously allied
to religious ritual, is a metaphor for change, an emblem of time
passing, and, in terms of dramatic structure, signifies character
development. It is a metaphor for the mental journey a
character must make in order to free himself from a sinful past
and be prepared for the inevitable reconciliation that comedy
requires.

Our response to Drusilla and her plight, however, depends
on our knowledge of her character presented in part through
the descriptions of other characters, but more importantly,
through soliloquy. Immediately prior to the recognition scene,
Drusilla alone on stage meditates on her situation. Having
discovered that her judgment of Lucrezio's infidelity is wrong,
she is disoriented and questions her own behavior. Her speech

manifests those features of dialogue so important to represent-ing the inner life. She asks herself a series of rhetorical questions about the past and her future behavior; she apostrophizes Lucrezio himself; she debates with herself about the future. Bargagli schematizes this division: 'L'un pensier mi dice: fuggilo, e l'altro mi dice: parlagli' (V, v, 24) ('One mind tells me, flee him; the other, speak with him'). She finally resolves to talk with Lucrezio to discover if he has maintained his faith. This soliloquy, which immediately precedes their reconciliation, dramatizes not only Drusilla's predicament by heightening the suspense, but also represents for us her divided mind.

As Clubb points out, Drusilla exemplifes the generic figure of the woman as wonder who possesses power as savior and benefactress, but she is also a character whose fate concerns us.[32] In *All's Well* and *Measure for Measure*, and later in *The Winter's Tale* in which the woman as wonder figure is unfolded into two characters, Paulina and Hermione, we find this figure of the heroine as instrument and representative of providence, who leads the hero to greater self-understanding through his admission of guilt and repentance. But we also find heroes and heroines whose characters have been subsequently the subject of generations of critical debate and analysis: Bertram and Helena, Angelo and Isabella, Leontes, Hermione and Paulina. Shakespeare found a providential structure and the generic figure of the woman as wonder in Italian drama; he also found there a rhetoric of character which helped shape his own portrayal of character in comedy.

Though Shakespeare's poetry distinguishes him both from his Italian predecessors who wrote in prose, and from his native models, with their rolling fourteeners, we cannot claim that his genius at manipulating the conventions of plot and character 'distinguishes Shakespeare's plays from all previous com-edies'.[33] Even Shakespeare's earliest attempts at romantic comedy distinguish him from such awkward native efforts as *Common Conditions* (1576), in which the morality tradition is uneasily, if humorously, allied with a romance plot filled with set speeches of self-revelation and Roman type characters, who engage in almost colloquial dialogue. But as *Gl'Ingannati* and its progeny demonstrate, the Italians had long since solved the problems inherent in dramatizing romance. Shakespeare inherited from his classical and Italian counterparts a body of dramatic and rhetorical materials long since successful on stage; he used and explored these dramaturgical conventions throughout his comedies.

6

'And all their minds transfigur'd': Shakespeare's early comedies

The Comedy of Errors, unlike most ancient and Italian comedies based on mistaken identity, depends on an accident, the *lusus naturae* of twins, rather than on contrivance or intrigue. Coleridge claimed that this difference distinguished farce from comedy and his judgment has long influenced critical evaluation of the play. Farce, most critics agree, subordinates character to plot and action, and *The Comedy of Errors* is generally read and played as farce. Its plot, we are told, invites preoccupation with action rather than with character. Since in the criticism of Shakespeare, characterization continues to be a primary criterion of evaluation, *Errors* must be, as the traditional judgment has it, 'apprentice-work, a typical remaniement of a Plautine original'.[1]

Such a view, however, ignores the play's poetry which invites interest not solely in its action, but in its characters, in Antipholus of Syracuse and Adriana, the other twin's unhappy wife. Poetry endows these characters with an inner life which holds our attention and makes the fate of Antipholus of

Syracuse significant and important. We want him to find himself through union with Luciana and his family. Shakespeare's emphasis on the character of the traveling brother represents the most fundamental change he works on his Plautine original; instead of focusing on the settled, householding sibling, Shakespeare concentrates on Antipholus of Syracuse's quest for his lost twin. Whereas Plautus presents us with two characters 'sufficiently alike so that each may fit interchangeably into the other's situation', Shakespeare creates two different characters whose behavior in response to similar errors and cross-purposes reflects their individualized selves.[2]

The most obvious formal difference between the two and also the most important for our purposes is that the traveling brother is given a series of soliloquies, whereas the resident brother has none. The first of such speeches comes in I, ii, immediately after the frame scene with Egeon and reveals a character wholly different not only from both Plautus' twins, but from Antipholus of Ephesus as well:

> He that commends me to mine own content
> Commends me to the thing I cannot get.
> I to the world am like a drop of water
> That in the ocean seeks another drop,
> Who, falling there to find his fellow forth
> (Unseen, inquisitive) confounds himself.
> So I, to find a mother and a brother,
> In quest of them, unhappy, lose myself.[3]

(I, ii, 33–40)

In the past twenty years *Errors* has inspired renewed interest in readers who have recognized in the play themes and techniques which Shakespeare uses throughout his dramatic career, not necessarily *in ovo*, but exploited with a sureness of dramatic understanding and skill characteristic of his later comedy.[4] Critics interested in the play often begin with this soliloquy in which Antipholus betrays a residual sense of self which persists beyond his function in the plot. The speech initiates the play's theme of identity, and if *Errors* is indeed Shakespeare's earliest comedy, these lines mark the beginning of a central paradox of the problem of identity and self-knowledge as Shakespeare treats it: Antipholus of Syracuse will 'find' himself, like Charisios and Knemon in Menander or Flamminio in *Gl'Ingannati*, by 'losing' himself.[5] He is searching not simply for a lost brother, but for his own identity. In recognizing man's smallness and insignificance through the famous water-drop image, Antipholus communicates his own isolation from his fellows and the sense of confusion and loss of identity which the play investigates.[6] Throughout the play Antipholus' lines, particularly his monologues, reveal his deepest fear, a loss of self conveyed through his preoccupation with and fear of change, a major theme and pattern of imagery in *Errors*.[7]

Antipholus of Syracuse and his Dromio part company immediately before this speech: Dromio goes in search of an inn with his master's money; Antipholus decides to explore the town. Shakespeare's handling of this parting is a skillful preparation for the comic business to follow, namely the first error, in which Antipholus of Syracuse mistakes Dromio of Ephesus for his servant and demands his money. Confronted with the very loss of self which he believes necessary to finding his family, Antipholus clings doggedly to his gold, a tangible object on which he feels his identity depends. In his second soliloquy following this farcical interchange, Shakespeare establishes the depth of Antipholus of Syracuse's anxiety over the loss of self so resignedly described earlier in the scene. The fears Antipholus voices about Ephesus are not simply that it is filled with conycatchers and dissemblers, or that its magic will 'deceive the eye', but that 'dark-working sorcerers' and 'soul-killing' witches will 'change the mind', and 'deform the body' (I, ii, 98 ff.). Though this nexus of imagery derives from ACTS XIX, Shakespeare links it carefully to the theme of identity which he explores in this play.[8] What Antipholus fears most is change and transformation of the self, not material or physical harm.

This transforming power becomes increasingly identified with women – with Luciana and the Abbess, and in a different way, with Adriana. Her long speech in II, ii about marriage, based on the neo-Platonic notion of the marriage bond as transforming two into one, states explicitly the theme of identity: 'O how comes it,/That thou art then estranged from thyself?' (II, ii, 119–20). Adriana describes marriage with the neo-Platonic figure, extending Antipholus' water-drop image when she argues that marriage is the confounding of self in the 'breaking gulf'; nor can the drop which is individual man be recalled 'unmingled'. Antipholus threatens throughout the action to escape Ephesus, to 'be gone the sooner', but he cannot depart before 'confounding'[9] himself both in marriage and in his family.

After the confrontation with Adriana we find one of those monologic speeches which, without being strictly an aside, is nevertheless outside the dialogue structure of the scene:

> What, was I married to her in my dream?
> Or sleep I now, and think I hear all this?
> What error drives our eyes and ears amiss?
> Until I know this sure uncertainty
> I'll entertain the offer'd fallacy.

> (II, ii, 182–6)

Confronted with two women both of whom seem to know him and question the identity he believes to be his, Antipholus of Syracuse responds with a monologue cast as dialogue at just that moment in the plot when his sense of identity is questioned. We find the series of rhetorical questions characteristic of such speeches which set up the I/you dichotomy of dialogue. The switch from the first to third person, from 'I' to 'our', as in Angelo's soliloquy in *Measure for Measure*, includes the audience in the errors and mistakes which Antipholus experiences. The inverted syntax of 'sleep I now' and the oxymoron 'sure uncertainty' signal an unhomogeneous structure of answer and response. Even this short speech reveals many of the features of dialogue which we have remarked upon in earlier soliloquies and monologic fragments, from Menander and Latin comedy through the Italian Renaissance plays. Such rhetoric serves to convey the quality of an inner life so often said to distinguish Shakespeare's characters from those of his predecessors.

Antipholus speaks these lines early in the action, but unlike Angelo, he has made no unexpected discovery about his inner nature. Consequently he questions the senses, first his own in the opening lines, then those of others. This significant difference – Angelo's preoccupation with internal experience, Antipholus' with external 'error' of sense impressions – suggests the direction in which Shakespeare developed the comic soliloquy.

This scene shows us, nevertheless, Antipholus' changing view of his circumstances. Though he wonders if he might be dreaming or sleeping, he is basically secure in his conviction of self. He will only 'entertain' a 'fallacy'. By the end of the scene, however, Antipholus seriously questions his identity:

> Am I in earth, in heaven, or in hell?
> Sleeping or waking, mad or well advis'd?
> Known unto these, and to myself disguis'd,
> I'll say as they say, and persever so,
> And in this mist at all adventures go.
>
> (II, ii, 212–16)

Unlike the stolid Antipholus of Ephesus who never doubts his identity but only assumes others are drunk or mad, Antipholus of Syracuse questions himself. Shakespeare uses rhetorical schema to represent his divided mind: antitheses (line 213), anaphora, and chiasmus (line 214). In Angelo's speech we also find antithesis, but its two halves fall in different lines, de-emphasizing formal rhetorical balance; the less schematic structure better communicates the nuances of Angelo's complex psychological state. These lines show Antipholus learning that identity depends at least in part on others' conceptions of him: on self, but as Adriana has suggested in her speech, on other as well.

The play does not merely imply that Antipholus changes. Shakespeare is very explicit in having the traveling brother describe himself as changed and re-created. Like so many Shakespearean protagonists, Antipholus is changed by his relationship with his beloved, Luciana. Through her for the first time he is able to see change and transformation in positive terms:

> Are you a god? would you create me new?
> Transform me then, and to your power I'll yield.
>
> (III, ii, 39–40)

Luciana, like Bargagli's Drusilla, is identified with the divine, and hers is a positive transforming power rather than the witchcraft and cozenage identified elsewhere in the play with Ephesus and its inhabitants. Antipholus has recognized the lesson of Adriana's earlier words; he sees in love and marriage a union of two in one which he makes explicit in this scene:

> It is thyself, mine own self's better part,
> Mine eye's clear eye, my dear heart's dearer heart,
> My food, my fortune and my sweet hope's aim,
> My sole earth's heaven, and my heaven's claim.
>
> Call thyself sister, sweet, for I am thee.
>
> (III, ii, 61–4, 66)

Loss of self in the other, Luciana, whose name means light, enables Antipholus to find himself, but here the process is not complete. Though he accepts the other in the person of Luciana, he continues to ignore the rest of the world: Luciana's continuing assertion of his duty to Adriana and his own search for his brother and mother. Like the lords of *Love's Labour's Lost*, or Romeo, or Orlando before he is educated by Rosalind – all Shakespearean lovers for whom love is self-absorption, dramatized by their excessively Petrarchan language – Antipholus describes his feelings in strikingly hyperbolic terms:

> Sing, siren, for thyself, and I will dote;
> Spread o'er the silver waves thy golden hairs,
> And as a bed I'll take thee, and there lie,
> And in that glorious supposition think
> He gains by death that hath such means to die;
> Let love, being light, be drowned if she sink.
>
> (III, ii, 47–52)

Luciana, a realist like so many of Shakespeare's heroines when confronted by such vows, cries 'What, are you mad that you do reason so?' Through love for Luciana Antipholus will confound himself once more. As a siren, she lures sailors to their deaths. *Death* here puns on the sexual meaning: he will embrace death encountered through her. Such self-dramatization and preoccupation with the rhetoric of love is always criticized by Shakespeare; he never allows love so presented to reach fruition.[10] It must either be tempered and educated to accommodate a larger world than that of the lovers alone or else end in tragedy.

Dromio's entry on the scene and his description of Luce with its bestial imagery is an effective counterbalance to Antipholus' idealizing love. Dromio undergoes a parallel transformation. He also questions his identity, asking 'Do you know me sir? Am I Dromio? Am I your man? Am I myself?' (lines 72–3). Instead of a lover, he becomes an ass. Seen through the sobering lens of Dromio's descriptive powers, Luciana is no longer divine, but a 'witch' who is 'possessed', whom Antipholus must escape 'lest myself be guilty to self-wrong' (line 162). He must rediscover his family and be reconciled to the world of Ephesus before he can find himself and be united with Luciana. To Antipholus of Syracuse, identity ultimately depends upon society: *esse* is *percipi*.[11]

At iv, iii Antipholus of Syracuse responds to one more confusion on Dromio's part,

> This fellow is distract, and so am I,
> And here we wander in illusions —
> Some blessed power deliver us from hence!
>
> (IV, iii, 40–3)

We do not see him again until his mother the Abbess, another woman with transforming power, delivers him from the maze of error in which he has confounded himself. Both literally and figuratively, Antipholus of Syracuse, the stranger and traveler of the play, unlike his twin, is willing to recognize he is 'distract'. This willingness to question himself makes him susceptible to change and leads him back to his family and to love.

But without Antipholus of Syracuse, whose speeches suggest his inner life, the play becomes the 'intricate impeach' the Duke describes in the final scene. We become more preoccupied with the action and the unraveling of errors, as in farce, than with the characters, because the character whose poetry best conveys his inner life is missing from the action. But even so Shakespeare continues the imagery of change and transformation through his emphasis on madness and Dr Pinch's exorcisms, and in the Duke's words 'I think you all have drunk of Circe's cup' (V, i, 271). When the errors are explained, Antipholus of Syracuse tells Luciana, 'What I told you then,/I hope I shall have leisure to make good,/If this be not a dream I see and hear' (374-6). Making good his understanding of her positive transforming power depends on the Abbess's revelation, which at last permits his integration into the society of Ephesus – another significant change Shakespeare works on his Plautine model. In Plautus, the resident brother goes off to sell all and return to Epidamnum with his twin. In Shakespeare, Antipholus of Syracuse is integrated into the society of Ephesus through family and impending marriage.[12]

Themes of change and transformation permeate *The Comedy of Errors*; when coupled with the rhetoric of consciousness found in the comic soliloquy or aside, we have the impression of a character's inner life and realistic development. Like *Errors*, *A Midsummer Night's Dream* is filled with imagery of change and metamorphosis, but when we go to the play in search of soliloquies or fragments of monologue which present a mind in conflict, self-conscious about such change, we are mostly disappointed. As G. K. Hunter remarks, the 'psychological dimension of inner debate is not one that this play employs'.[13] The lovers, though aware of having undergone a profound experience, have no self-consciousness about its meaning or implications. The fairy world itself is in some ways less an objective force in the plot than an almost allegorical rendering of the lovers' mental lives, a making literal of the conflicts love engenders.

Readers have often remarked that the lovers are virtually indistinguishable,[14] but their speeches reporting their experiences to Theseus at IV, i, when looked at closely, offer more than is usually admitted. Lysander's lines (IV, i, 145 ff.) are filled with hesitations, parenthetical elements, and inverted syntax which represent a mind struggling with a profoundly disturbing experience not entirely ordered or understood. Demetrius' long account which follows does not portray conflict, as represented in Lysander's speech, but simply reports his actions and aims in going to the wood. His words convey little sense of struggle or self-examination; he is content to explain his change of heart by means of 'some power' (line 164). In the short dialogue which follows, the imagery of sight so important to the *Dream*, with its double meaning of vision or insight, returns to play a central role in the lovers' interchange and report of their experience. Instead of the immediacy which characterizes Bottom's account of his dream, to the lovers the events of the night are distorted, 'small and undistinguishable,/Like far-off mountains turned into clouds', and 'double', seen with 'parted eye' (IV, i, 186–9).[15] Demetrius' lines (lines 191–4) which follow display the rhetorical questions and allusions to dream characteristic of Antipholus' speech, but here such features are not set apart from the dialogue in order to suggest inner confusion. Instead of the first person singular, Demetrius casts his questions in the plural and speaks for all the lovers.

Shakespeare downplays the lovers' responses to their experience, subordinating them to another dramatic purpose: to emphasize Bottom's soliloquy which ends the scene. By deliberately minimizing the immediacy and self-consciousness of the lovers' reflections, Shakespeare saves the dramatic moment for Bottom's struggle to put his experience into language: his cue has come, and he answers it. Having learned how to manipulate the conventions for rendering conscious-ness, here Shakespeare plays with those strategies, endowing Bottom rather than his lovers with a speculative inner life – Bottom the ass, with his malapropisms, stubborn literalness and stolid imperturbability in his relations with his fellows and the fairies. Ironically he has the most perceptive and telling moment of revelation in *A Midsummer Night's Dream*. In his soliloquy we hear his mind moving through the experiences of the night, taken aback by their fantasy and improbabilities, for once in the play almost at a loss for words. Caught up in the night's implausibilities, even Bottom is incredulous. His sense of having had a vision, his broken prose lines which represent the stumbling movement of his mind over the night's events, the careful rhetorical repetitions juxtaposed with his mixed metaphors of biblical allusion, all play with what I have termed the rhetoric of consciousness, parodying its strategies so as to show the irony of the woodland fantasy and to intimate the lovers' limitations. His soliloquy also bespeaks his artistic aspirations, for he wants to order his experience into song. Act IV, i is peculiar in that it leaves hanging two such moments, promised but never represented. The lovers exit pledging that along the way they will recount their experiences to Theseus and Hippolyta; similarly Bottom promises to sing 'Bottom's Dream' before the Duke at the end of Pyramus and Thisbe, as a kind of coda, it would seem, and commentary on the lovers' tragedy.[16] But we never hear either Bottom's dream transformed into song or the lovers' accounts of their nocturnal adventures.

Though part of the subplot, Bottom nevertheless figures as a comic protagonist in *A Midsummer Night's Dream* because of his central role in bringing about the reunion of Oberon and Titania. When they 'are new in amity' (IV, i, 86) all of the other characters can at last resume their proper identities and be themselves reunited with their appropriate mates. Many Shakespearean clowns have soliloquies, such as Launce's to his dog, or Costard's lamenting his remuneration, but their set speeches have little relation to the main plot's developing action. By endowing one of his plebeian characters with an inner life, by presenting Bottom as more sensitive, however garbled and comic, in his understanding and desire to memorialize the woodland adventure, Shakespeare links Bottom with his comic fellows in the later comedies who, however more self-conscious and witty, use language to subvert social, political or sentimental hierarchies.[17] Vain and ignorant, Bottom's exuberance and histrionic desires help him make an imaginative leap we never see the lovers make. Only Hippolyta recognizes in the lovers' jointly recounted, if offstage, tales of love's power, 'minds transfigur'd' (V, i), rather than mere 'fancy's' images; we have no sense that they are self-conscious about the changes wrought by their adventures. On the contrary, their responses to the mechanicals' interlude witness a devaluation of the power of imagination and a corresponding over-valuation of what cool reason comprehends.

As in *A Midsummer Night's Dream*, so in *Love's Labour's Lost* 'reason and love keep little company together' (III, i, 138–9). Each of the courtiers discovers the truth of Berowne's claim that their vow to study in retreat is out of season. In the wonderfully dramatic scene in which each lord discovers his love and is discovered by his fellows, finally Berowne himself, whose downfall we have awaited with amusement and a sense of inevitability, is exposed. All the lords are transformed by love and forced to recognize their essential humanity: 'We cannot cross the cause why we were born' (IV, iii, 214).[18] But that change is presented comically, with no attempt to represent mental conflict. Indeed, part of the scene's comic effect depends on the very superficiality and lack of conflict or reflection in those changed allegiances, from the contemplative to the active life.

In *Love's Labour's Lost*, as in later sixteenth-century Italian comedy, symmetry precludes sympathy. Here the love of women is not the individual human passion Shakespeare dramatizes in his love comedies, but a mating game. When the ladies trade favors so that each lord woos the wrong beloved, the lords, 'Following the signs, woo'd but the sign of she' (v, ii, 469). This line sums up the behavior of the courtiers and accurately characterizes how language functions in the play. The elaborate puns, quibbles and word-play between Moth and Armado, Berowne and the others, Boyet and the ladies, among the lords and ladies themselves, all illustrate Shakespeare's use of language to further the theme of error and misunderstanding. The characters delude themselves with their own language: the lords with the heroic style of proclamation and vows, and later with Petrarchanism; Armado by his stereotypical boasting and absurdity; Holofernes by his learning and pedantry. Synecdoche, one of the play's most frequent figures, mirrors the minds of the characters, particularly the lords who continually mistake the part for the whole.

One speech of Berowne's, however, deserves analysis. In this short soliloquy immediately preceding the revelation scene, Berowne discovers his love quite differently from the subsequent revelations of his fellows. Instead of sonneteering, we have Berowne speaking his only prose speech in *Love's Labour's Lost*. Though he uses prose in dialogue with Costard and Armado, all his major speeches but this one are in verse so rhetorically gaudy and elaborate as to obscure any sense of self-revelation. Here, however, prose works by contrast to reveal his thoughts more openly than elsewhere in the play:

> The king he is hunting the deer; I am coursing myself: they have
> pitched a toil; I am toiling in a pitch, – pitch that defiles:
> defile! a foul word. Well, set thee down, sorrow! for so they
> say the fool said, and so say I, and I the fool: well proved,
> wit! By the Lord, this love is as mad as Ajax: it kills sheep, it
> kills me, I a sheep: well proved again o' my side! I will not
> love; if I do, hang me; i' faith, I will not. O! but her eye, – by
> this light, but for her eye, I would not love her; yes, for her
> two eyes. Well, I do nothing in the world but lie, and lie in
> my throat. By heaven, I do love, and it hath taught me to rhyme,
> and to be melancholy; and here is part of my rhyme, and here my
> melancholy. Well, she hath one o' my sonnets
> already: the clown bore it, the fool sent it, and the lady hath
> it: sweet clown, sweeter fool, sweetest lady! By the world, I
> would not care a pin if the other three were in. Here comes
> one with a paper: God give him grace to groan!
>
> (IV, iii, 1–19)

The opening metonymic shift from factual statement, 'The king is hunting the deer', to 'I am coursing myself', in which Berowne substitutes an aspect of the hunt, 'coursing', for the hunt itself, and then puns on the word, which also meant 'to turn over in one's mind', admirably moves the audience into Berowne's mind. The paranomasia which follows, built on the contrast between what the other lords are doing and what Berowne is feeling, suggests associative thought. Unlike other soliloquies we have considered, Shakespeare does not use rhetorical questions here – in fact, though we have several indicators which suggest dialogue, the dialogue seems less with the self than with an imagined interlocutor, the subjects of the imperatives 'set thee down' and 'hang me'. This imaginary dialogue is first with 'sorrow', whom Berowne addresses, and then with 'wit', which might suggest inner debate, but here suggests rather a praise of Berowne's witty proof, more self-congratulation than self-examination. In the following lines, he in fact moves from wit which proves, to address his 'side'. The imperative, 'hang me', though certainly a means of self-address, creates an independent listening persona more than a sense of Berowne's conscience or inner self. The movement from sorrow to fool to Berowne himself, and from Ajax to killing sheep to Berowne again, suggests not only his quick wit, but also his degraded attitude toward love, reminding us of his earlier verse soliloquy in III, i, in which he imagines himself as the signor junior, giant dwarf, dan Cupid's corporal and Rosaline as a German clock. The very self-consciousness with which Berowne calls attention to his rhetorical flourishes emphasizes that he is a man of surfaces whose mind works more in tropes than in schemes. This short dialogue with self dissolves into the traps of Petrarchanism which have ensnared the other lords, the shift marked by the antistrophic repetition of eyes, and the allusions to riming and melancholy. Our momentary glimpse into Berowne's mind is cut off by the codified language of love. If *Love's Labour's Lost* is about finding a language which communicates love, Berowne, like his fellows, never seems to find the proper accent, rhythm or substance.

Love's Labour's Lost presents a social model of language in which meaning is determined within a context by the auditor as well as the speaker, just as identity is determined within social relationships and material conditions as well as by the self. Language and identity are relative, dependent at least in part on the world outside rather than on the self within.[19] The courtiers, represented by Berowne, are unable to escape from the disguise language represents. When he attempts honest plain words, his speech is as elaborate and conceited as ever.

Rosaline and the other ladies decry this insincerity and require each lord to prove his love over time. Berowne claims that the ladies are responsible for their lovers' false vows. His religious language, 'sin', 'purifies', and 'grace', though it suggests the pattern of sin, confession and regeneration characteristic of Shakespeare's late comedies and romances, and of the *commedia grave*, seems just one more disguise, a conceit rather than a deepened conception of past action and future behavior. We never have a sense in *Love's Labour's Lost* that the characters have learned from their experiences or that an inner life governs their behavior, for the symmetry of the action reminds us forcibly that we watch a play.

The rhetorical features common to Shakespeare's comic soliloquies share features with set speech soliloquies of self-revelation characteristic of early Elizabethan romantic comedies such as *Common Conditions* and *Clyomon and Clamydes*. Typically in these early plays a scene ends with a resumé of the action and a presentation of the character's state of mind. In the case of Antipholus' or even Bottom's soliloquies, their speeches do both. But the way in which they accomplish these tasks is quite different from the set speeches of *Clyomon and Clamydes* and *Common Conditions*. Take, for example, the first few lines of Neronis' soliloquy in which she is converted to loving Clyomon. The plot is based on the fourteenth-century prose romance *Perceforest*, and this speech begins with a poem or song 'How can that tree but withered be/That wanteth sap to moist the root?' The soliloquy proper begins accordingly as follows:

> *Neronis*, ah I am the Tree, which wanteth sap to moyst the roote.
> *Neronis*, ah I am the vine, whose Plants are troden under foote.
> I am the spray which doth decay, and is with wild weeds
>   overgrowne,
> I am the wight without delight, which shows, and hath no good
>   wil showne.
> Mine is the heart by whom alas, each pleasant joy doth passe,
> Mine is the heart which vades away, as doth the flower or grasse.
> In wanting sap to moyst the roote, is joyes that made me glad,
> And plants being troden under foote, is pleasures that was had.
> I am the spray which doth decay, whom cares have overgrowne,

But stay *Neronis*, thou saist thou showest, and hath no good
    will showne:
Why so I do, how can I tell, *Neronis* force no crueltie
Thou seest thy knight endued is, with all good gifts of courtesie:
And doth *Neronis* love indeed, to whom love doth she yeeld,
Even to that noble brute of fame, the knight of the golden
    Sheeld.
Ah wofull Dame, thou knowest not thou, of what degree he is,
Of noble blood his gesters showe, I am assured of this.
Why belike he is some runnagate that will not show his name,
Ah why should I this allegate, he is of noble fame.
Why dost thou not expresse thy love, to him *Neronis* then?
Because shamefastness and womanhood, bids us not seek to
    men.[20]

(xi, 1002–21)

The fourteeners themselves, with their rigid regularity,
unrelieved regular placement of the caesura and consequen-
tially deformed syntax, are a far cry from colloquial speech and
an unlikely medium for conveying any sense of 'lifelikeness'. The
line length and rhythm, the rhetorical repetitions, the internal and
end rhymes, the romance diction and stereotypes, the endless
apostrophes, all work to emphasize the soliloquy as artifice, a
rhetorical set piece not designed to individualize character.
The romance set speech tends to generalize rather than
problematize feeling by likening the heroine's situation to that
of countless other young women in similar circumstances of
unrequited love. However, Shakespeare situates such speeches
in particular contexts with temporal markers, demonstrative
pronouns and other features, as we have noted in Angelo's and
Antipholus' soliloquies. Indeed we might say that far from
demonstrating an inner life or character in excess of function,
such speeches reveal characters as absolutely determined by
their function in the romance or intrigue plot. Unrequited love,
contemplated suicide, tragic discovery, and the like all have
within the romance tradition conventional metaphorical commonplaces and generalized tropes for conveying those gener-
ically-bound experiences. Neronis' soliloquy, despite its devices of self-address, is paradoxically univocal; it expresses an
idea, the discovery of love, from a single point of view.

If we turn to a representative soliloquy from *The Two Gentlemen of Verona*, in which Valentine mulls over his loss of Silvia, we find a kind of middle ground between the romance set piece and the strategies of self-revelation we have remarked in other Shakespearean comic protagonists:

> And why not death, rather than living torment?
> To die is to be banish'd from myself,
> And Silvia is myself: banish'd from her
> Is self from self. A deadly banishment.
> What light is light, if Silvia be not seen?
> What joy is joy, if Silvia be not by?
> Unless it be to think that she is by
> And feed upon the shadow of perfection.
> Except I be by Silvia in the night,
> There is no music in the nightingale.
> Unless I look on Silvia in the day,
> There is no day for me to look upon.
> She is my essence, and I leave to be,
> If I be not by her fair influence
> Foster'd, illumin'd, cherish'd, kept alive.
> I fly not death, to fly this deadly doom:
> Tarry I here, I but attend on death,
> But fly I hence, I fly but away from life.[21]

(III, i, 170–87)

The rhetorical questions indicate inner debate, but as in *Clyomon*, we find no specifying links to the preceding scene – no temporal markers or demonstrative pronouns, and no attempt to problematize Valentine's response to his experience. We also find the predictable diction, antitheses, and motifs of romance, rhetorically repeated, throughout: separation from the lover is likened to death, the beloved is all joy, light, nightingales, influence and essence. Such commonplaces generalize rather than individualize Valentine's feelings.

In his suggestive study of Boccaccio, H. J. Neuschäfer analyzes the shift from the medieval *exemplum* to the new stylistic principles of the *novella*. He argues that *exempla* such as the generous friend who gives his own beloved to his friend, the rudimentary plot of *The Two Gentlemen of Verona*, is problematized in the *novella* because 'the characters, instead of being simply the means for illustrating an idea, possess a conscience'.[22] The ideal of friendship and magnanimity is challenged by the constraints of the real – the more complex and reflective character of the friends themselves, and the beloved who refuses her status as an object. Boccaccio's Sophronia possesses a conscience and unleashes a series of complications which problematize the *exemplum*, making it unruly, difficult to moralize.

This schema and description of the relation of *exemplum* to *novella* is useful in considering the relation of romance and early romantic comedies such as *Common Conditions* or *Clyomon and Clamydes* to the later comedies of Shakespeare. Shakespeare problematizes character in his comedies by endowing his characters with what we have termed a rhetoric of consciousness; he organizes soliloquies and monologic fragments as dialogue and complicates the relation of character to context by features of style such as colloquial verse forms, caesuras and breaks in thought which counter end rhymes and iambic rhythm, and by diction which counterpoints the predictable language of romance or tragedy. The soliloquy organized as dialogue provides a means for dramatizing the inner life of a given character, a means for creating that residue or excess which remains with us and makes Shakespeare's characters seem complex and lifelike. But we find the fullest use of the convention of mistaken identity and the rhetoric of consciousness to develop comic character in his later romantic comedies.

7

Magic versus time:
As You Like It
and *Twelfth Night*

As You Like It, by its contrasts, illuminates Shakespeare's use of the rhetoric of consciousness. Here we learn about Rosalind and the other characters not through self-revelation in soliloquy, the basic strategy of the New Comic model, but through their interaction with other characters and the contrasting of one attitude with another, of Touchstone's physicality with Silvius' pastoral laments, for example. In fact, the play has only one soliloquy, which closes the first act, in which Oliver expresses his hatred of Orlando. Though Shakespeare has Rosalind use asides to juxtapose her true feelings with her assumed pose as critic of love, these remarks are always addressed to another character, usually Celia. And because Rosalind's disguise is self-consciously assumed, it does not lead to the kind of confusion and suffering experienced by the Antipholi in *Errors*, or by Bottom and the lovers in *A Midsummer Night's Dream*.

Despite the play's dearth of soliloquies or monologues which manifest a rhetoric of consciousness, we inevitably experience Rosalind as a complex character. Readers of *As You Like It* generally agree that the play is about testing and education.[1] Rosalind's disguise is intentional; she uses it to expose the conventional postures of love which the other characters assume, to educate Orlando, Silvius and Phoebe to less idealized and less self-dramatizing passions.[2] In the process, Rosalind moves back and forth between two identities, as Rosalind and as Ganymede, and in doing so she is educated herself.[3] Sexual disguise brings about this education, but at those moments in the play where self-address and the rhetoric of consciousness might generate in the audience a sense of the inner workings of Rosalind's mind, instead Shakespeare distances us from his characters through scenes of dialogue, through formal, highly stylized language, and through miraculous or supernatural events.

Consider first the scene in which Rosalind is exiled by Duke Frederick. Instead of leaving Rosalind alone on stage to lament her plight in soliloquy, Shakespeare advances the action through a scene of dialogue with Celia. And we should note that Rosalind does not begin as the gallant and powerful impresario of action whom we later encounter in Arden. When Celia insists on following her and suggests they seek refuge in the forest, Rosalind responds in a stereotypically feminine manner:

> Alas, what danger will it be to us,
> Maids as we are, to travel forth so far?
> Beauty provoketh thieves sooner than gold.[4]

(I, iii, 104–6)

Celia, undaunted, suggests disguise, and Rosalind develops Celia's plan by proposing to disguise herself as a man. Celia leads in this scene, not Rosalind, and it is she who speaks the famous lines, 'Now go we in content/To liberty, and not to banishment.' In the forest, Rosalind's language changes, but rather than show us a mind in conflict, Shakespeare has her adopt the linguistic stereotype of a man. Her first words are an oath, a testament to her masculine identity; she assumes the male role of Celia's comforter and exhorts her to courage. Though Shakespeare presents us with a changing Rosalind, we have no insight into how this change comes about other than through her mechanical assumption of masculine disguise and the linguistic stereotypes of male and female.

More important to *As You Like It* than the inner life are social games which lead the characters not to greater understanding of themselves, but to greater capacities for social interaction and harmonious commitments in love and marriage. Where we might expect to find Rosalind reflecting upon her plight, as at her discovery that Orlando is in the forest writing verses to his beloved Rosalind, Shakespeare reveals her feelings instead through dialogue with Celia and Touchstone. Her many questions are not rhetorical, as we have found so often in characters whose identities are threatened, but literal: 'What did he when thou saw'st him? What said he? How looked he? Wherein went he?' (III, ii, 216–17). At Orlando's appearance, she determines to 'speak to him like a saucy lackey' and proceeds to mock his declared love. Rosalind's love mockery, so different from her extravagant excitement, love sickness, and desperate inquiries to Celia, suggests for us her inner turmoil. What is missing is not a sense of her inner life or personal struggles, her capacity to hold the contrasting views of love she expresses in the play in a poised and balanced equilibrium, but rather self-consciousness about that equipoise expressed through soliloquy. Rosalind's inner debates are externalized in her role as Ganymede/Rosalind, and we are correspondingly distanced from her feelings, however much we may appreciate her character. We share the pleasures of flirtation, of transvestism, of shifting roles and playful irony, all of which testify to Rosalind's fascination by giving her dimensions in excess of her function. We are called upon to hold together, in the study or in performance, the multiple aspects of her character, but we never have the sense that she herself recognizes or struggles with that multiplicity.

Instead of a confessional soliloquy, when confronted with Oliver's highly stylized, almost allegorical tale of Orlando's heroism, Rosalind swoons. In the next scene, when Orlando refuses to continue their game and cries out that he 'can live no longer by thinking' (V, ii, 50), far from fearing the loss of Orlando's company and courtship, Rosalind claims miraculous powers given her by a magician: she promises to materialize Rosalind. Orlando reacts directly: 'Speak'st thou in sober meanings?' (line 69). Her response, however, both answers and evades. She reiterates her promise in language which hints, in its formal balance and repetitions at a magician's spell, ordering Orlando to prepare for the wedding, 'for if you will be married tomorrow, you shall; and to Rosalind if you will' (lines 72–4).

Rosalind's lines have only hinted at the formal and distancing rhetoric which follow. Each character in turn repeats the words of the preceding in response to Silvius' enumeration of 'what 'tis to love'.[5] It is almost as if the characters are under a spell or in a trance, and significantly, after another series of such repetitions, Rosalind breaks the spell, complaining that they all sound 'like the howling of Irish wolves against the moon' (lines 110–11), activity traditionally associated with strange happenings and mysterious, supernatural events.

In the final scene we find Shakespeare using once again the language of spells, vows and the like. It serves to emphasize the ritual festivities of marriage and harmony with which the play ends. The action is no longer directed and ratified by Rosalind, but by Hymen whose miraculous arrival or descent brings about the marital harmony of the play's finale. Whatever sense we might have of the characters' development or maturation is subordinated to a sense of magic and wonder.[6] Only in *As You Like It* and the late *Cymbeline* does Shakespeare use the device of the *deus ex machina* literally. The Abbess of *The Comedy of Errors*, the Duke of *Measure for Measure*, Paulina in *The Winter's Tale*, Prospero in *The Tempest*, all partake of the supernatural through the roles they play in the final scenes, but only in *As You Like It* among the early comedies does Shakespeare have a god speak and control the action on stage.

Rosalind's claims of magical powers and the incantatory, stylized and repetitive stichomythia of the two preceding scenes among the lovers prepare for Hymen's arrival and role in the action. The god of marriage's language continues what we

have already heard from the other lovers, but with the addition
of rhyme:

> You and you no cross shall part.
> You and you are heart in heart.
> You to his love must accord,
> Or have a woman to your lord.
> You and you are sure together,
> As the winter to foul weather.

(V, iv, 130–5)

Having given his blessing to each pair of lovers, Hymen
speaks a final quatrain to the assembled company:

> Whiles a wedlock hymn we sing,
> Feed yourselves with questioning,
> That reason wonder may diminish
> How thus we met, and these things finish.

(V, iv, 136–9)

The ensuing action, however, far from explaining away
wonder, intensifies it, for before Rosalind can utter a word of
explanation, the second and heretofore unintroduced brother
of Orlando and Oliver arrives to tell of yet another strange
miracle, the conversion of Frederick by 'an old religious man'.
We may remember here that Rosalind/Ganymede has told
Orlando that she owes her education to 'an old religious
uncle'. At III, ii when Rosalind speaks these lines the audience
believes them to be false. But at the end of the play, when we
hear of the 'old religious man' who converts Duke Frederick,
we are reminded of Rosalind's uncle who made a convert of her
as well; magic and wonder increase rather than diminish. Even
Jaques, whose satiric role has served to offer, along with
Ganymede's, a corrective view of life and love, speaks this
language of patterned, repetitive rhyming incantation:

> You to your former honour I bequeath,
> Your patience and your virtue well deserve it.
> You to a love that your true faith doth merit:
> You to your land and love and great allies:
> You to a long and well-deserved bed:

And you to wrangling, for thy loving voyage
Is but for two months victuall'd. So to your pleasures.
I am for other than for dancing measures.

(V, iv, 185–92)

Rosalind's prose epilogue breaks the magical spell which envelops the final action. Her words are designed to call attention to the play as play, to her role as actor, and thereby to dispel the sense of wonder which the finale conveys. This emphasis on magic links *As You Like It* in some ways more closely to *A Midsummer Night's Dream* than to *Twelfth Night* and *Much Ado* with which it is often grouped. Certainly *Twelfth Night* is a comedy in which wonder plays an important part, but in *Twelfth Night* wonder is associated with fortune, time and human action rather than with magic and the supernatural.

In *Twelfth Night* Shakespeare uses mistaken identity not only as a means of complicating the plot, but also as a figure for self-delusion, for the mistakes men make about themselves. Though the central mistakes in identity arise from Viola's disguise as Cesario and the eventual confusion between Cesario and Sebastian, there are also, as many readers have noted, the 'identities' created by the imagination: Orsino's as melancholy lover to Olivia; Olivia as mourner to her brother; Malvolio as lord to Olivia and her household; and even Sir Toby's fictitious version of Sir Andrew.[7]

Both Olivia and Orsino demonstrate the limits of their 'identities' by their erratic behavior, which they express primarily through language. In the course of his first six lines, the duke praises music as the food of love and then declares 'Enough, no more;/'Tis not so sweet now as it was before.'[8] He calls attention to his own irrational behavior, attributing it to the 'spirit of love' and equating love with fancy. So in II, iv, in his conversation with Viola, first Orsino affirms that like all true lovers he is 'Unstaid and skittish in all motions else,/Save in the constant image of the creature/That is belov'd (II, iv, 18–20). But following this avowal of constancy, and marked by the emphatic full stop in the middle of the line, is an abrupt change of subject: the question to Viola 'How dost thou like this tune?', a tune which we learn, ironically enough, helps to relieve his passion. Within fifteen lines he then contradicts himself when he affirms that instead of being constant, men's 'fancies are more giddy and unfirm,/More longing, wavering, sooner lost and worn/Than women's are' (lines 33–5).[9] And finally he tells Viola, 'Make no compare/Between that love a woman can bear me/And that I owe Olivia' (lines 102–4). As in so many of Shakespeare's comedies, the clown speaks truth; he affirms the duke's changeableness: 'Now the melancholy god protect thee, and the tailor make thy doublet of changeable taffeta, for thy mind is a very opal' (II, iv, 73–5).[10]

Some critics observe only the absurdity of Orsino and Olivia, but Shakespeare endows them with poetry which makes them sympathetic rather than ridiculous. If we compare Silvius' language in *As You Like It* with Orsino's, we can see that both lovers are preoccupied with the postures of the romantic lover. Silvius, however, is ridiculous because of the mechanical, imitative quality of his verse and actions. In his confession of love to Corin in II, iv, 30–9, Shakespeare parodies the rhetoric both of the Petrarchan and the pastoral lover. Silvius' mechanical series of 'if thou' clauses along with the monotonous repeated choral lines 'Thou has not loved' prevent our taking his feelings seriously. The same is true of his actions, for his abrupt departure crying Phoebe's name, which he carefully explains is caused by his passion, makes him absurd. For Silvius, love motivates predictable actions – folly, rehearsals of 'thy mistress' praise', and the lonely retreat from company. Orsino plays with the clichés and expected behavior of the lover in highly figurative verse, but he is not governed by them. For him, the postures of love provide tropes which he uses creatively, as in his imaginative reworking of the pun on hart in I, i, 19 ff. He plays self-consciously with the conventions – with the relation between love and music, with the analogy between love and the hunt, with mythological allusions – measuring the distance between himself and ideal romantic behavior. Despite his affectation, the quality of his poetry proves him a worthy lover to Viola.

Olivia also suffers from an unlimited imagination, first in creating her fictive identity as 'cloistress' and then, like Orsino, showing her changeable nature and unreadiness for love by loving the epicene Cesario. The clown exposes her 'disguise' as mourner in I, v, 50 ff. when he 'proves' her a fool, but her relation to Cesario is more complex. Again like the duke she recognizes something in Cesario which attracts her, but her feelings also betray a fear of marriage and adult love. Orsino has already described the ambiguous nature of Cesario's sexuality; Malvolio's description, which precedes their first meeting, emphasizes the page's effeminancy. Olivia's soliloquy at the end of the scene effectively conveys a sense of her inner life by revealing the change wrought in her by love:

> '... I am a gentleman.' I'll be sworn thou art:
> Thy tongue, thy face, thy limbs, actions, and spirit
> Do give thee five-fold blazon. Not too fast: soft! soft!
> Unless the master were the man. How now?
> Even so quickly may one catch the plague?
> Methinks I feel this youth's perfections
> With an invisible and subtle stealth
> To creep in at mine eyes. Well, let it be.
>
> (I, v, 295–302)

Shakespeare makes Olivia seem lifelike by casting her musings about Cesario's enigmatic responses about his parentage in dialogue; she uses rhetorical questions, self-address in the admonition to herself 'Not too fast: soft! soft!' and the caesura to indicate shifts in thought. The traditional courtly conceit of love's entering by the eyes, unlike Silvius' description of the events of courtly love, is personal – 'Methinks I feel' she says, eschewing hyperbole. Her willingness to accept love's transforming power ('Well, let it be') rather than lament it wins our sympathy and prepares us for her marriage to Sebastian. The final lines continue the courtly metaphor used to present Olivia's divided mind: she fears her eye is opposed to her mind. In *Measure for Measure*, Shakespeare gives us no inkling of what is to come of Angelo's discovery that he desires Isabella, but he is careful to establish and confirm our comic expectations for Olivia's love. The lady resigns herself to fate rather than human agency, but she is willing enough to help fate along by sending Cesario her ring. More important is the immediately following scene in which we learn Sebastian is alive and well, knowledge which reassures us that the comic confusion of Olivia's love for the disguised Viola will be resolved happily.

Disguise and wooing by proxy are nevertheless dangerous business. Viola's beauty, sincerity, and particularly her description of how she would woo (I, v, 254 ff.), win Olivia's love. In her soliloquy which follows Sebastian's first scene we find many features of the rhetoric of consciousness we have noted in comedy:

> I left no ring with her: what means this lady?
> Fortune forbid my outside have not charm'd her!
> She made good view of me, indeed so much,
> That methought her eyes had lost her tongue,
> For she did speak in starts distractedly.
> She loves me, sure; the cunning of her passion
> Invites me in this churlish messenger.
> None of my lord's ring? Why, he sent her none.
> I am the man: if it be so, as 'tis,
> Poor lady, she were better love a dream.
> Disguise, I see thou art a wickedness,
> Wherein the pregnant enemy does much.
> How easy is it for the proper false
> In women's waxen hearts to set their forms!
> Alas, our frailty is the cause, not we,
> For such as we are made of, such we be.
> How will this fadge? My master loves her dearly,
> And I, poor monster, fond as much of him,
> And she, mistaken, seems to dote on me:
> What will become of this? As I am man,
> My state is desperate for my master's love:
> As I am woman (now alas the day!)
> What thriftless sighs shall poor Olivia breathe?
> O time, thou must untangle this, not I,
> It is too hard a knot for me t'untie.
>
> (II, ii, 16–40)

Rhetorical questions establish the I/you opposition characteristic of inner debate, as do the semantic reversals of antithesis ('As I am man ... As I am woman'), and the inserted parenthetical elements which convey the confusion Viola feels. But because she understands full well how the mistakes have come about, Viola does not fear madness or believe she dreams. It is Sebastian, her other self, who is subjected to those aspects of mistaken identity, who believes he is mad or dreaming.

Shakespeare divides Viola's speech into three distinct sections. The first ten lines comment upon the preceding interchange with Olivia. They include a mirror passage in which Viola describes and interprets Olivia's gestures and behavior; their function is essentially reportorial.[11] Viola's apostrophe of 'Disguise' marks the second section. She shifts from the first person singular to the plural to extend her audience much as Angelo does in *Measure for Measure*. But whereas Angelo's pronoun shift signals his recognition of a shared humanity, Viola's transfers responsibility for her predicament from herself to her sex and its alleged susceptibility to Satan's inventiveness. Though she personifies disguise, Viola attributes Olivia's confusion and her predicament not finally to a supernatural power, but to human nature, or more precisely, women's 'frail' natures. And because she captivated Olivia without guile, she does not believe herself responsible for the consequences of her disguise. In the soliloquy's final section, Viola rehearses the complications of the intrigue. Shakespeare emphasizes Viola's comic plight and her sexual ambiguity through the alternating pronouns, the 'I' versus 'him' (line 33) and 'she' versus 'me' (line 34), and through the succeeding lines which describe her situation as man and as woman. In a final rhyming couplet, Viola decides to let time untangle the knot her love has tied. Both Olivia's and Viola's willingness to give over control, to count on fate or time rather than themselves or magic, distinguish them from the powerful Rosalind.

Critics since Johnson have found Olivia's marriage to Sebastian hard to accept. E. M. W. Tillyard, in discussing the bed trick in *Measure for Measure*, complains of *Twelfth Night*:

it may be useful to ask why popular opinion has objected to the bed trick and not objected to something equally disgusting in *Twelfth Night*, namely Olivia's accepting Sebastian as a substitute lover for Cesario. The idea that Viola and Sebastian had interchangeable souls is a monstrous insult to human nature.[12]

What Tillyard and others forget is that Olivia does not fall in love with Cesario's soul, by which I take him to mean personality or inner nature, but with his 'perfections' which crept in through her eyes. The quality of her love is not undermined by winning the appearance of the man she loves, for his identity all along is subsumed in what Viola/Cesario calls her 'outside' (II, ii, 17). Through that outside Olivia has 'insight' into Sebastian's nature and identity. The epicene figure of Cesario can be compared to a *trompe l'oeil* perspectivist painting. When Olivia sees him from her point of view, she 'sees' Sebastian; when Orsino looks at Cesario, he 'sees' Viola. The figure of Cesario illustrates the ambiguous Renaissance attitude toward the verbal-visual problem which fascinated poets and theorists alike.[13] Cesario's 'outside' is both an accurate and a mistaken reflection of reality; his sexual ambiguity embodies both twins and neither.

One of the recurring themes of the play is whether or not appearance reflects the true self. In her first scene Viola speculates on the captain's inner nature:

> And though that nature with a beauteous wall
> Doth oft close in pollution, yet of thee
> I will believe thou hast a mind that suits
> With this thy fair and outward character.

> (I, ii, 48–51)

Later in III, iv, Antonio mistakes Cesario for Sebastian and is rebuffed. He laments that 'to his image, which methought did promise/Most venerable worth … Thou hast, Sebastian, done good feature shame.' Though 'a beauteous wall/Doth oft close in pollution', the action of the play argues that outward appearance finally reflects inward truth, even in the complex case of Cesario. To fault Shakespeare's conception of identity in human relations by saying that they are reduced to physical appearance alone is to ignore the importance in the Renaissance of appearance as a speaking picture of the inner self. Such an attitude was no doubt influenced by widely diffused neo-Platonic doctrines which taught that visible beauty bespoke hidden reality. Throughout the sixteenth century and certainly in Shakespeare there is an uneasy trust in the relationship between the visual sign and its inner meanings, if one is initiated, like Viola, into the rites of 'seeing'. Viola's role is to lead both Olivia and Orsino to recognize in Cesario what they seek in love.

Sebastian's response to Olivia, his faith and generosity, prove him a worthy partner in marriage. To Sebastian, the world of Illyria seems strange and fantastic. Like Antipholus of Syracuse, he thinks he is mad or dreaming, motifs associated with mistaken identity as we have seen throughout classical and Renaissance comedy. But unlike the mistakes of *The Comedy of Errors*, the error, the content of the 'dream', answers his true and natural desires. He recognizes that he is neither mad nor dreaming in the free act of giving himself to Olivia.[14] Like other characters whose identities are mistaken – the Antipholi, Sosia – he asserts the reality of sense experience: 'This is the air, that is the glorious sun,/This pearl she gave me, I do feel't, and see't' (IV, iii, 1–2). Like so many of Shakespeare's comic characters, he must lose himself to find his true identity as husband to Olivia. The wonder that Sebastian declares 'enwraps me thus' is quite different from the madness of *Errors* or the magic of *As You Like It*. It is not a controlling impresario of action who brings about Sebastian's marriage to Olivia, but his willingness, so similar to that of Olivia and Viola earlier, to accept what comes.[15]

Many readers have seen in Malvolio a satirical portrait of the puritan or melancholic, or a foil whose delusions parody the delicate or rowdy aberrations of the court characters. But since Lamb's essay 'Oh Some of the Old Actors', some critics have claimed Malvolio as a tragic figure who learns from his error.[16] Certainly Shakespeare endows him with an inner life in his series of revealing monologues, but unlike the other characters for whom the rhetoric of inner debate suggests conflict, struggle and development, Malvolio's soliloquies are diffused in various ways to emphasize Malvolio's unselfconsciousness. He neither questions his own behavior nor is willing to abandon reason to rely on time or fortune to resolve his predicament.

Shakespeare creates for Malvolio an inner life that consists of little more than fantasies of wish-fulfillment in which he imagines himself lording it over Olivia, Sir Toby and his cohorts. In II, v, Malvolio enters in soliloquy:

> 'Tis but fortune, all is fortune. Maria once told me she did
> affect me, and I have heard herself come thus near, that
> should she fancy, it should be one of my complexion.
> Besides, she uses me with a more exalted respect than any
> one else that follows here. What should I think on't?
>
> (lines 23–8)

These lines come at a time in the play that allows us to judge whether or not Malvolio's reflections correspond with his actions and character thus far presented. We have seen Olivia in I, v, chastise him for his 'self-love' and 'distempered appetite' and our memory of her words discredits his claim that she treats him with 'a more exalted respect'. We are amused by his fantasy that Olivia's wanting a lover of a melancholy temperament means she fancies him. The rhetorical question which ends the passage would seem to initiate an inner debate, establishing the I/you oppostion of dialogue we have elsewhere analyzed. But, in what follows, the role of interlocutor is taken over by the eavesdroppers, and Malvolio's soliloquy, instead of inner debate, becomes stage dialogue. Malvolio, far from questioning himself, immediately takes off into his social and sexual fantasy of 'Count Malvolio'. That fantasy is questioned of course, not by a created inner self, conscious of the discrepancy between an imagined reality and the lived world, which in his view ('There is example for't') serves only to confirm his desires, but by the outraged comments of Sir Toby, Andrew, Fabian and Maria. The fantasy becomes a dialogue with Sir Toby, not with conscience or self. Like Berowne in *Love's Labour's Lost*, Malvolio's interlocutor is not the self. But whereas for Berowne, an imaginative created persona and his own rhetorical inventiveness prevent self-analysis, for Malvolio it is prevented by the limits of his egotism and by the dramatic scene itself in which he gets his come-uppance from the eavesdroppers' malicious commentary.

When Malvolio finds the forged letter, his responses parody the parallel speech of Olivia's that we have already considered in which she discovers her love for Cesario. Instead of mental movement back and forth as she struggles with newly discovered feelings, the forged *billet-doux* simply confirms what Malvolio has just been fantasizing. His *softly* (line 122) and *soft* (line 142), parallel Olivia's in I, v, 297, but far from holding him back or suggesting conflict and the need for caution, they are linked to moments of impetuosity. At line 122, *softly* leads to his discovery of the anacrostic on his name, and at line 142 *soft* leads on to the text of the letter itself about which he exclaims after having read it, 'Daylight and champaign discovers not more! This is open.' To Malvolio, everything, every action, every silence, every gesture, is self-evident, generates no debate, and can only serve to confirm his already firm good estimate of himself. Far from suggesting development or change, Malvolio's monologue here simply emphasizes what we already know of him; he is full of self-love. So also in his next soliloquy at III, iv, 64 ff. in which the dialogue is not with the self, but with the letter. In a moment of unwitting self-revelation he gloats 'nothing that can be can come between me and the full prospect of my hopes'. Certainly not good sense, self-doubt, a sense of decorum or of social place.

Malvolio's seriousness and the recognition of his exclusion from the harmonious finale of *Twelfth Night* are intimations of a tragic possibility which Shakespeare develops more insistently in *Much Ado* and the so-called problem comedies. Malvolio has affinities with Bertram in *All's Well*. Both are male lover-protagonists, though Malvolio merely parodies that character function. Bertram is reclaimed by the requirements of the comic love plot, but as generations of audiences have admitted, we feel dissatisfied because of his refusal to learn from his experiences, by Shakespeare's stubborn insistence that he fails to change. Both Bertram and Malvolio infuse the final acts of their respective plays with bile – whether in Malvolio's threats to be revenged, or in Bertram's shrewd boggling (V, iii, 232). Both refuse to be reformed by the comic action, and both have been given enough character, enough of that residue or excess we have identified with Shakespearean characterization, to leave us uncomfortable. Already in Malvolio's portrayal in *Twelfth Night*, though subdued and unemphasized by his subsidiary role, refuses us the simple pleasure we might take in a comic butt or stereotype. In *Twelfth Night* we have already a hint of the discomfort audiences have so often complained of in the portrayal of Claudio in *Much Ado*, and of Angelo in *Measure for Measure*.

8

Mistaking in *Much Ado*

Many readers of *Much Ado About Nothing* have remarked that its tragicomic pattern sets it apart from Shakespeare's other romantic plays and links it with the so-called problem comedies. I want to turn finally to *Much Ado* because it brings us full circle to *Measure for Measure*. Unlike the threatened tragedy of *Measure for Measure*, however, the tragedy of *Much Ado* is apparent rather than real. Things appear to happen; all the characters at one moment or another are seduced into believing in appearances, and its two plots are linked by this common theme of credulity and self-deception. Readers of both plays have been troubled by the uneasy union of vehement and lifelike passions with the conventions of comedy, in *Much Ado* in IV, i, and in *Measure for Measure* in the shift from the first three acts to the last two. Of *Much Ado*, J. R. Mulryne complains that 'the unlovable Claudio is too vividly and realistically portrayed (in the manner of a figure in tragedy)'.[1] Tillyard argues of *Measure for Measure* that the change to the conventions of comedy from the 'more lifelike passions is too violent' and that the bed trick is not a 'case of modern prudery unaware of Elizabethan preconceptions but of an artistic breach of harmony'.[2] Shakespeare's persistent use of substitution, disguise and the language of mistaken identity in both plays establishes from the outset comic expectations in the audience which are ultimately fulfilled, but as Jean Howard has recently argued of *Measure for Measure*, the play

> strains and distorts a comic paradigm Shakespeare had used many times before, and in so doing calls attention to the way in which any set of conventions, generic or otherwise, can betray its basic function of mediating between audience and author to create lifelike illusions and becomes instead a sterile mechanism inadequate to its task.[3]

She goes on to claim that *Measure for Measure* is an experiment in which Shakespeare attempts to escape from conventional comic formulas without losing his audience's 'power to comprehend'. Though I find this view persuasive, I would like to qualify it by suggesting that the 'problem' of *Measure*, and that of *Much Ado* as well, is not so much the inadequacies of art and its conventions 'to create a satisfactory illusion of lifelike complexity', but the uneasy union of the traditional comic plot designed to call attention to artifice, coincidence and wonder, with the conventions of realistic characterization, particularly the rhetoric of consciousness. In *Much Ado*, IV, i, and in *Measure for Measure*, Shakespeare uses such conventions so forcefully that our willingness to accept the artifice of their comic plots is undermined. Instead of extending the metaphorical power of mistaken identity by shifting its emphasis from plot to character, from external to psychological or internal mistaken identity, Shakespeare undermines our comic expectations by exaggerating the conventions of lifelike characterization in these plays. In *Much Ado*, Claudio is presented as a type common to Shakespeare's comedy, the courtly lover, but in IV, i, Shakespeare endows him with an inner life which conflicts with the type. So also in *Measure for Measure* the conventions of realistic characterization Shakespeare uses in portraying Angelo and Isabella conflict with the Duke's intrigue plot. The 'problem' of the two plays is not real passions versus comic conventions, as is so often claimed, but two kinds of opposing conventions, one which calls attention to itself and its artifice, the other which conceals itself by seeming 'real'.

There are, of course, obvious differences between the two plays which make the labels romantic comedy and problem play appropriate. *Much Ado* does, after all, have the strictly comic plot of Beatrice and Benedick, which embraces rather than disapproves of sexuality; it has Dogberry and the watch strategically placed to assure us that all will be well instead of the problematic Duke whom Lucio slanders and whose improvisations with Ragozine's head seem uncomfortably forced. And *Much Ado* ends with the marriage of its lovers, not with a judgment scene in which the Duke calls for and administers an Old Testament vengeance to Lucio and proposes marriage to the silent Isabella. But we need to look first at Shakespeare's portrayal of Claudio before we can compare *Much Ado* and *Measure for Measure* and assess their similarities and differences.

In *Much Ado*, Claudio mistakes Hero's true nature, discovers his error, and believing it has caused Hero's death, must atone for his 'sin'. Mistaken identity provides the means whereby both the mistake and Claudio's subsequent development is communicated to the audience. Like so many comic heroes, Claudio must lose in order to find. This fundamental pattern, which we have seen elsewhere, is juxtaposed with Beatrice and Benedick's parallel discovery of their mutual love.

Claudio's character, like Angelo's, has always seemed to trouble readers of *Much Ado*. Cynics claim he woos Hero for her money;[4] romantics counter that his query about Leonato's family stems from timidity and embarrassment.[5] It is perhaps anachronistic to fault Claudio because he asks about Hero's financial expectations, for even the cynical Benedick believes his friend's devotion is real. But our discomfort with Claudio's repudiation of Hero in the church scene is less easily dismissed. Before we consider IV, i, however, we need to look at how

Shakespeare introduces Claudio and establishes the romance plot.

The play's first lines present Claudio as the courtly ideal: 'he hath borne himself beyond the promise of his age, doing, in the figure of a lamb, the feats of a lion: he hath indeed better bettered expectation' (I, i, 12–15).[6] His falling in love with Hero is equally conventional. Before she utters a word, he loves her, and though not at first sight, from the moment of seeing her after his return from the wars. His language is that of the courtly lover: 'In mine eye, she is the sweetest lady that ever I looked on' (lines 174–5). He asks 'Can the world buy such a jewel?' (line 168), and as his verb suggests, he betrays a mercantile attitude toward love. Claudio needs assurance that others value his 'jewel of price' and seeks confirmation of his love from Benedick.

Don Pedro's offer to woo Hero for Claudio triggers the first 'suppose' of the play. A servant overhears this conversation, reports it to Leonato, who then believes Pedro woos Hero for himself. Claudio in turn believes Don John's tale of Pedro's love for Hero so that the action of the masked ball, as many have noted, prepares for the villain's intrigue by demonstrating Claudio's credulity and lack of self-confidence. His excessive idealism, untempered by compassion or by the sense of play which characterizes Beatrice and Benedick, explains how he can be duped by Don John's disguise plot. Though he participates in the game of gulling the two would-be lovers, he hasn't the imagination to include play in his own lovemaking.

John Anson argues that the balcony scene is a fantasy enactment of Claudio's own fears and subconscious desires which he displaces on to the object of his idealized passion.[7] Just as Don Pedro indulges Beatrice and Benedick in a fiction which corresponds to his own secret wishes, so his brother Don John indulges Claudio in a vision of his ambiguous desires: a lustful Hero whose sexuality both attracts and repels. The vehemence of Claudio's public slander, his 'public accusation' as Beatrice condemningly calls it, testifies to that same excess of passion which made him idealize his beloved. Claudio has no sense of human weakness and therefore responds with selfish cruelty to the disappointment of his imagination. His world is an imaginative construct which has encompassed reality by halves – only its romance and none of its frail humanity. His sense of self is so dependent on his imagined ideal vision of love that when that vision is disappointed, his own identity is threatened. We in the audience are doubly aware of his lack of human compassion because we know Hero is falsely accused. Her 'sin' endangers him because on some level it corresponds with his own repressed desire.

Neither the historical argument that the Elizabethans expected such a public repudiation, nor the attempts to excuse the count's behavior at the church on the grounds of a lofty idealism and disgust toward sexuality, exonerate Claudio. Most readers agree with Chambers that 'Claudio stands revealed as the worm that he is'.[8] His rejection of Hero is somewhat roundabout, a combination, it would seem, of his own desire for a shocking revelation and the bystanders', particularly Leonato's, ignorance. Shakespeare casts the opening interchange into the 'plain form of marriage' so that Claudio seems to comply with a code even in his repudiation. When the friar asks if he comes 'to marry this lady', the count says no, but he is interpreted by Leonato to be quibbling over the way in which Friar Francis poses the question. Claudio lets this interpretation stand. After another such exchange, he takes over from the friar and proceeds with the ritual forms himself, but his questions are as misleading as his earlier responses. His ambiguous question at IV, i, 26–7, with its ironic reference to Hero as 'this rich and precious gift', and Pedro's similarly deceptive response, allow Leonato once again to misinterpret his intentions. Finally, Claudio openly repudiates his bride, but his compliance with the ritual forms of the ceremonial occasion confirms our sense of the count's character as bounded by conventional codes.[9]

Having returned Hero to her father, Claudio's anger and passion break forth. The emphasis shifts from the ceremonial occasion and its ordained participants – priest, father, bride and groom – to Hero herself. The demonstratives ('*this* rotten orange, *that* blood, *these* exterior shows') and the appeals to the audience ('Behold,' 'all you that see her') bespeak the count's determination to achieve an effect. Again Leonato misinterprets Claudio's words, for he believes the young man himself to have 'made defeat of her virginity'. Claudio's claim of bashful sincerity and comely love brings Hero's innocent but unfortunate reference to 'seeming', which prompts his passionate denunciation. Critics have noted the similarity between Claudio's language here and that of Hamlet and Othello:[10]

> Out on thee, seeming! I will write against it.
> You seem to me as Dian in her orb,
> As chaste as is the bud ere it be blown;
> But you are more intemperate in your blood
> Than Venus, or those pamper'd animals
> That rage in savage sensuality.
>
> (IV, i, 56–61)

Claudio focuses in these lines on Hero rather than the assembled audience, a change which makes his feelings seem more intensely personal and less determined by forms and codes. Shakespeare uses the rhetoric of consciousness to endow Claudio with an inner life that breaks the confines of literary convention and ceremonial decorum. Instead of the courtly lover of the previous action, he becomes an individual of psychological complexity whom we both pity and despise.[11] His description of Hero is based on the paradoxical contrast between what she seems and what he knows she is: 'Her blush is guiltiness, not modesty' (IV, i, 41). The irony is that the opposite is true, for what 'seems', is, and what he 'knows', is false. As in earlier speeches in which we find such rhetoric creating an inner self, paradox and antithesis represent Claudio's divided mind. Though addressed to Leonato, the series of questions beginning at line 69 are rhetorical and establish the pronominal contrast between 'I' and 'you'. They also situate Claudio firmly in the moment and the real world, a necessary feature of dialogue. The count makes of Hero two persons, a Diana and a Venus, 'most foul, most fair' (line 103), and this divided Hero represents in language the poles of his

own divided self. His lament, 'O Hero! What a Hero hadst
thou been' betrays genuine emotion.[12] Here he is oblivious to
family and friends, preoccupied with feelings, not forms. From
an excess of idealism in love, Claudio is transformed into a
suspicious misogynist who knows himself no better than
before. Until he learns how he has been deceived, he cannot
know himself, recognize his failures, and love properly.

Friar Francis restores sanity and reason to the impassioned
scene of denunciation by recognizing Hero's honesty and by
proposing still another 'suppose', her feigned death. He argues
the fundamental comic perspective of losing to find:

> for it so falls out
> That what we have we prize not to the worth
> Whiles we enjoy it, but being lack'd and lost,
> Why then we rack the value, then we find
> The virtue that possession would not show us
> Whiles it was ours: so will it fare with Claudio
> When he shall hear she died upon his words,
> Th'idea of her life shall sweetly creep
> Into his study of imagination,
> And every lovely organ of her life
> Shall come apparell'd in more precious habit,
> More moving-delicate and full of life,
> Into the eye and prospect of his soul
> Than when she liv'd indeed: then shall he mourn –
> (IV, i, 217–30)

The friar understands that Claudio has loved the idea of Hero;
when the count learns of his mistake, he says 'Sweet Hero!
Now thy *image* doth appear/In the rare semblance that I
lov'd it first' (V, i, 245–6, emphasis added). Friar Francis
expects to transform Claudio's imagination and lead him to a
more just judgment of Hero, but the 'idea of her life' never has
time to 'sweetly creep/Into his study of imagination'.

Immediately following the scene in which Claudio learns of
Hero's death, Benedick gives his challenge. Critics have been
disturbed by the jesting in this scene, but Claudio's callousness
would not claim our attention had Shakespeare not set up
expectations for his development which are never met. Friar

Francis' prediction that the count will mourn Hero 'though he thought his accusation true' leads us to expect a repentance like Flamminio's in *Gl'Ingannati* where Lelia's beloved condemns his past behavior even before he learns of her love and loyalty. Even more important, our sense of Claudio's inner life, of his passionate disappointment, genuine emotion and divided mind, leads us to expect a different, more feeling response to the news of Hero's death. Though there are sound theatrical reasons for delaying Claudio's response to the more dramatic moment of confrontation with Leonato after Borachio has confessed the crime, the count's heartlessness is troubling because it fails to fulfill our expectations for the comic plot.

If we compare Shakespeare's presentation of Claudio with that of Beatrice and Benedick, we can see how he extends the convention of mistaken identity to add depth and interest to their characters, but without transgressing the carefully defined limits of their comic plot. In Benedick's soliloquy in II, iii, immediately preceding the eavesdropping scene, Shakespeare presents a character already aware of love's transforming potential. Speculating on Claudio's transformation, Benedick remembers how his friend had once 'no music with him but the drum and the fife, and now had he rather hear the tabor and the pipe' (lines 13–15). He questions his own identity, wondering whether he may 'be so converted and see with these eyes?' 'Yet I am well', he repeats, trying to convince himself. The modal verbs he uses are *shall* and *will*, not *should* and *would*, future rather than subjunctive; his language betrays his openness to loving Beatrice.

Pedro, Leonato and Claudio present Benedick with the strong evidence of Beatrice's attachment he needs to admit his love. The deceivers spend very little time talking of Benedick's scorn. Instead, they recount the signs of Beatrice's love: she is up twenty times a night to write to him, beats her heart and tears her hair. Hero even fears she may do herself harm. They wish Benedick 'would modestly examine himself, to see how much he is unworthy so good a lady' (II, iii, 200–1). And that is exactly what he does. The ease with which Benedick is 'converted', or in the language of the play, 'caught', makes it clear how close to the surface his love has been: 'Love me? Why, it must be requited' (lines 215–16). In his previous soliloquy he asks 'can I be so converted'; here he has been converted indeed. Benedick is willing to change: 'Happy are they that hear their detractions and can put them to mending.' His vision altered by knowledge of Beatrice's love, Benedick now begins to interpret her differently. What was once judged quarrelsome is now thought loving. His notion of himself and of her has changed, and consequently her words have different meanings.

Despite this change, his character still conforms to the broad outlines of a comic stereotype, the *miles gloriosus*.[13] His boasting of success with women and his martial reputation connect him to the *miles* tradition just as Claudio's language and actions have connected him to the tradition of the courtly lover. After the slander of Hero, when he and Beatrice admit their love, Benedick's avowals imply his martial talents: 'By my sword, Beatrice, thou lovest me', (IV, i, 272) and 'I will swear by it that you love me, and I will make him eat it that says I love not you.' But unlike the Plautine braggart, Benedick is truly a martial hero and his engagement to Beatrice to fight Claudio is real. In Benedick Shakespeare has created an individual character who is also a comic type, a talent for which we should remember Donatus and other commentators praise Terence.

The deceit of Beatrice presents a very different fiction. Hero and Margaret emphasize not Bendick's love, but Beatrice's disdain. They exaggerate her scorn for the opposite sex, describe her derision of a man's love and compliment Benedick's worth and valor. Their fable portrays a Beatrice whose wit protects her from emotional involvement. The deceits perpetrated by the other characters satisfy the individual needs of each lover: Benedick's fragile ego needs the safety of Beatrice's love in order to admit his own; Beatrice's fear of male domination makes her scorn love. Her soliloquy, like Benedick's, is filled with rhetorical questions, paradox, and the juxtaposition of past, present and future, all features of dialogue. But there are significant differences in the two lovers' speeches. Beatrice speaks in verse, and the shift to poetry, the first she uses in the play, marks the liberation of her desire. Whereas Benedick wonders whether he can change and love Beatrice, she questions whether or not he loves her. Their individual responses bear out the differences in the way they are gulled: Benedick through his self-love; Beatrice through her 'wild heart' which makes her fear domination by men.

Even with these visions of the other's affections, however, it takes the heightened emotion of the church scene, an impossible moment for their usual self-protective repartee, for Beatrice and Benedick to let down their defenses and admit their mutual love. When Leonato tells them they were 'lent eyes to see', he telescopes the way in which the play juxtaposes mistaken identity with mistaken insight. Mistaken identity, role-playing and alternate identities are therapeutic instruments which lead the characters to self-knowledge, for these comic devices are not simply tools for developing plot, but springboards for experimentation whereby men and women escape from self-delusion to the self-understanding which enables them to live and love.

Comic decorum, which dictates the lovers' conversion to love, also prohibits Claudio's being made into a tragic figure who undergoes a psychologically 'real' development. He cannot, argues M. C. Bradbrook, be 'allowed more than a pretty lyric by way of remorse'.[14] Critics have claimed that Claudio's behaviour can best be understood within the context of a Decameron-like story, but as we have seen in IV, i, Shakespeare endows him with a psychological complexity in excess of what such a plot requires.[15] No reading of the play can excuse the brutality of his treatment of Hero, but the conventional comic action does demand that he be forgiven.[16] When he learns of his mistake, Claudio asks of Leonato, 'Impose me to what penance your invention/Can lay upon my sin; yet sinn'd I not/But in mistaking' (V, i, 267–9). But for Shakespeare, mistaking is enough; the play asserts that the sins of ignorance and credulity have consequences as dire as Don John's sins of will. Claudio's explicitly religious penance at Hero's tomb, though only sketched, is a conventional means of dramatizing his movement through sin and confession to repentance and self-knowledge. Though certainly a 'pretty lyric', Claudio's lines also unite *Much Ado* with the dark comedies and late romances in their emphasis on ritual forgiveness.

Much Ado About Nothing richly deserves the frequently drawn comparison with *Measure for Measure*. Just as the intensity of Angelo's appetite for Isabella and her vehement rejection of her brother's plea to live threaten our sense that comic conventions are adequate to our experience of that play, so Claudio's repudiation of Hero in the church scene, and his intractable unwillingness to conform to Friar Francis' comic vision of losing to find, trouble our satisfaction with *Much Ado's* comic resolution.

In both *Much Ado* and *Measure for Measure*, the careful balance between the conventions of comic plotting and those of lifelike characterization which Shakespeare maintains in his earlier comedies is upset. The rhetoric of consciousness which he employs adds depth and complexity to his comic characters and to the convention of mistaken identity, extending it from a plot device to a means of representing character development on stage. This inner life receives an emphasis more characteristic of tragic than of comic drama. In the criticism of tragedy, comic intrusions were once called 'comic relief', but both the pejorative term itself and its correspondingly reductive view of such scenes in tragedy have been rejected in favor of a larger claim for the tragic vision, its expansiveness and complexity. A similar prejudice has troubled the criticism of Shakespeare's comedies, and to a limited extent those of his predecessors. Too often, critics have judged his use of a deliberative mode of comic characterization as a kind of bumbling intrusion of the tragic into comedy, whether in terms of Renaissance readers and audiences such as Sidney and Jonson, who labeled such plays 'mongrel tragicomedy', or modern Shakespeareans who criticize Claudio's outburst in the church scene, or the problematic generic status of *Measure for Measure*.

Angelo is, of course, more interesting and complex a poetic creation than Claudio. In part this difference can be explained in simple quantitative terms – Angelo has a much greater portion of the lines and share in the action of *Measure for Measure* than Claudio has in *Much Ado*, in which the displacement of the main plot maintains our sense that the 'ado' is about 'nothing'.[17] But there are more significant differences. Shakespeare's portrayal of Claudio as courtly lover is less interesting than that of Angelo as ascetic and judge. Angelo is not bound by the conventions of type character which Shakespeare found so useful in creating Claudio and making his gullibility believable. Most important, of course, is Angelo's self-consciousness, the recognition of his own shortcomings and failures which Shakespeare renders so vividly in the soliloquies in II, ii, 167 ff. and later in II, iv, 1–30. By making Angelo self-conscious about his desire for Isabella, by having him debate its merits and consequences, Shakespeare creates a complex comic character who arrests our imaginations.

Generic complexity is a feature of Shakespeare's dramatic practice, and as Rosalie Colie has argued, of Renaissance habits of reading and writing generally.[18] Many have remarked that the comedies and romances contain within them tragic actions;[19] recently, Shakespeareans have identified comic matrices in the great tragedies.[20] I have argued that the generic boundaries of characterization are as flexible in Shakespeare's dramaturgy as those of plot and structure; because he often uses deliberative strategies common to tragic characterization within the dramatic boundaries of his romantic comedies, we perceive his comic characters as complex and lifelike.

9

Shakespeare's rhetoric of consciousness

The being of men is founded in language. But this only becomes actual in conversation.

(Heidegger, 'Holderlin and the essence of poetry')

If Claudio and Angelo have often been compared with Shakespeare's tragic protagonists, it might be useful finally to turn to a character from the great tragedies, to analyze a tragic soliloquy proper to discover shared features of style and rhetorical play which link the comic and tragic soliloquy and demonstrate the conventions of realistic characterization which I have argued characterize Angelo and Claudio's speech.

Perhaps no character of Shakespeare's plays has been more often noted for his self-consciousness, for his inner life, than Hamlet. The multiplicity of Hamlet's mind has indeed often been said to account for his tragedy – his indecisiveness, his recognition of the conflicting claims of the subjective self and the objective world. Without pretending to address the interpretive problems of *Hamlet*, a task which the limits of this study preclude, I would like nevertheless to look at a particular soliloquy of *Hamlet* in order to illustrate the conventions of realistic characterization and the portrayal of the inner life which I have shown so far only within the generic boundaries of comedy.

In II, ii, after the player's speech on the death of Priam, Hamlet in soliloquy attacks his cowardice and inaction in a speech which manifests all the features of dialogue we have elsewhere analyzed, and creates the effect of a mind in conflict with itself through what I have termed a rhetoric of consciousness:

> Ay, so, God buy to you. Now I am alone.
> O what a rogue and peasant slave am I!
> Is it not monstrous that this player here,   545
> But in a fiction, in a dream of passion,
> Could force his soul so to his own conceit
> That from her working all his visage wann'd,
> Tears in his eyes, distraction in his aspect,
> A broken voice, and his whole function suiting   550
> With forms to his conceit? And all for nothing!
> For Hecuba!
> What's Hecuba to him, or he to her,
> That he should weep for her? What would he do
> Had he the motive and the cue for passion   555
> That I have? He would drown the stage with tears,
> And cleave the general ear with horrid speech,
> Make mad the guilty and appal the free,
> Confound the ignorant, and amaze indeed
> The very faculties of eyes and ears.   560
> Yet I,
> A dull and muddy-mettled rascal, peak
> Like John-a-dreams, unpregnant of my cause,
> And can say nothing – no, not for a king,
> Upon whose property and most dear life   565
> A damn'd defeat was made. Am I a coward?
> Who calls me villain, breaks my pate across,
> Plucks off my beard and blows it in my face,
> Tweaks me by the nose, gives me the lie i'th' throat

As deep as to the lungs – who does me this?   570
Ha!
'Swounds, I should take it: for it cannot be
But I am pigeon-liver'd and lack gall
To make oppression bitter, or ere this
I should ha' fatted all the region kites   575
With this slave's offal. Bloody, bawdy villain!
Remorseless, treacherous, lecherous, kindless villain!
Why, what an ass am I! This is most brave,
That I, the son of a dear father murder'd,
Prompted to my revenge by heaven and hell,   580
Must like a whore unpack my heart with words
And fall a-cursing like a very drab,
A scullion! Fie upon't! Foh!
About, my brains. Hum – I have heard
That guilty creatures sitting at a play   585
Have, by the very cunning of the scene,
Been struck so to the soul that presently
They have proclaim'd their malefactions.
For murder, though it have no tongue, will speak
With most miraculous organ. I'll have these players   590
Play something like the murder of my father
Before mine uncle. I'll observe his looks;
I'll tent him to the quick. If a do blench,
I know my course. The spirit that I have seen
May be a devil, and the devil hath power   595
T'assume a pleasing shape, yea, and perhaps,
Out of my weakness and my melancholy,
As he is very potent with such spirits,
Abuses me to damn me. I'll have grounds
More relative than this. The play's the thing   600
Wherein I'll catch the conscience of the King.[1]

                                             (II, ii, 543–601)

   The soliloquy may be divided conveniently into six sections
or movements, each representing a shift in Hamlet's thought.
In the first, to line 566, Hamlet compares his real situation with
the imagined conceit of the player whose impassioned
performance moves Hamlet; the second movement suggests
self-examination *per se*. Hamlet, having moved away from his
analysis of the player's response and comparison of it to his

own, now looks inward at his own situation, which he conceives as a challenge or affront; this self-contemplation breaks off at line 571 in swearing, which leads him to compare himself to a whore; finally at line 584 we have the plan for the presentation of the Murder of Gonzaga, and the logical move thereafter at line 594 to questioning the spirit itself to determine whether or not it is an agent of the devil sent to bring about Hamlet's damnation. Each shift of thought takes place in the middle of the line; similarly, each rhetorical question in the first section is not end stopped, but breaks the rhythmic line. Such pauses heighten the naturalistic over the poetic, suggesting interrupted thought by playing the pattern of thought against the poetic line.

Shakespeare establishes a dialogue with self emphatically in the second half of Hamlet's opening line, 'Now I am alone.' The self-accusing apostrophe 'O, what a rogue' constitutes the speech as inner debate, and what follows is appropriately an extended rhetorical question which establishes the I/you dichotomy characteristic of dialogue. By casting the opening description of the player in the interrogative mood, Shakespeare avoids the distancing reportorial dimension such a description might otherwise create. The shift in line 544 to modal verbs 'should', 'would' (lines 554, 556) from the opening descriptive movement establishes the judgmental tone of self-recrimination that characterizes the soliloquy until Hamlet formulates his plan. We also find many of the features of dialogue we have remarked in earlier Shakespearean soliloquies, the demonstrative pronouns and adverbs, temporal markers and verb tenses which connect these lines to the preceding players' scene. The first half-line, for example, assumes Rosencrantz's goodbye, and the 'this' and 'here' in line 545 refer emphatically to the player who has just enacted the death of Priam. Later in line 574 'ere this' situates the audience by reminding us of the time passed since old Hamlet's appearance to his son. The 'this slave' which follows requires us to supply the antecedent to understand the reference to Claudius in the series on 'villain' which follows.

As in Angelo's speech with which we began, the most

complex aspect of dialogue, what Mukařovský calls semantic reversals, suggests the unhomogeneous relation of speakers in a dialogue. Such reversals are manifested in lexical oppositions and logical jumps of many kinds. In the first section of Hamlet's speech, we have not only a general opposition established between Hamlet and the player, but a further contrast between the player as Hamlet ('had he the motive') and the 'general ear' which is also divided into a series of opposing groups, the 'guilty' who are made mad/the 'free' who are appalled; the 'ignorant' who are 'confounded'/those 'faculties' which are 'amazed'. The allusion to the 'general ear' of course, draws us as audience into the debate – into what category do we fall? And the allusion to making mad the guilty recalls the decision already taken to enact the Gonzaga interlude and foreshadows the extended explanation of Hamlet's plan which follows. The rhythmically disruptive adversative, 'Yet I', emphasizes the opposition between Hamlet and the player which he goes on to elaborate from his own rather than the player's perspective.

The diction in this speech is intentionally low, in part certainly to convey Hamlet's psychological state, his self-denigration, but also I think to ensure a realistic or naturalistic balance to the tone of melodrama or high tragedy. Shakespeare juxtaposes words such as *rogue, peasant slave, muddy-mettled rascal, John-a-dreams, pate, tweaks, swounds, pigeon-liver'd, ass, drab,* and *scullion,* to the heightened language of *passion, distraction, heaven, hell, soul,* and *malefactions.* The soliloquy becomes, in Bakhtin's formulation, 'a dialogically agitated and tension-filled environment of alien words, value judgments and accents'.[2] Hamlet's name-calling (*rogue, peasant slave, John-a-Dreams, ass*) here is oddly incongruous with the sweet prince's character as it has so far been presented, and particularly in the immediately preceding conversation with the players and Polonius. Such language represents Hamlet's perception of self, an imagined relation to his situation not justified by logic or reason; the names are correlatives which communicate Hamlet's state of mind rather than describe his person or behavior. Both Angelo's metaphors and Hamlet's self-recrimination are designed to communicate their emotional states. Here also, as in Angelo's speech, we find the aposiopetic interjections, *Ha, Foh,* and *Hum* which emphasize mental conflict.

Though emphatically distinct in their substance – revenge versus desire – Hamlet's and Angelo's soliloquies manifest shared rhetorical features and organization. But Hamlet's soliloquy differs from Angelo's speech, for unlike Angelo, whose soliloquy is an inner debate of the divided self, with the I and you of dialogue represented directly in self-address ('What art thou, Angelo?'), Hamlet creates scenarios, addressing himself indirectly in his name-calling and in his imagined roles as player, challenged or insulted party, whore, and finally melancholic. He plays parts even in his mind. Hamlet's dialogic and histrionic imagination paralyzes him, inhibits action simply by the multiple possibilities his imagination offers and which Shakespeare here represents rhetorically.

As Harry Levin has observed, in this soliloquy Hamlet 'ponders not only the technique of acting, but the actual nature of the aesthetic process'.[3] Hamlet meditates on the relationship of the player to the play, but perhaps more interesting for our purposes is the implied question about characterization this soliloquy poses: how can being and emotion be communicated dramatically? The soliloquy has a metadramatic dimension in its exploration of the problem of how character is expressed on stage, not only through gesture and physical presence, but through spoken language.

We began this study with the problem of characters as beings, and in closing we might return to the problem of being from a slightly different, but nevertheless suggestive perspective. In his essay 'The influence of language on the development of scientific thought', Cassirer makes the following observations:

> For Aristotle, it has long been recognized that the particular categories of being he distinguishes are closely related to the categories of language and grammar. Aristotle's theory of categories sets out to describe and determine being to the extent to which it is somehow made explicit and analyzed according to the different forms of the enunciations. But all enunciating requires first of all a

subject to which it can be connected, a thing about which one expresses a predicate. Therefore the category of being is placed at the head of the theory of categories. Aristotle defines this being [ousia] in a sense that is both ontological and linguistic. ... The unity of *physis* and *logos* appears thus in Aristotle's system not as accidental but as necessary.[4]

In the *Categories*, Aristotle sets out to describe being as it is expressed, or 'the ways of saying being'.[5] Though the categories of thought Aristotle names are not homologous with linguistic categories, there is a remarkable congruence between the questions of rhetoric – the *sitne, quid sit* and *quale sit*, the predications which can be made about a debate or controversy, or for legal or dramatic purposes, a character – and the categories of thought he enumerates in the *Organon* and the *Metaphysics*.

Cassirer, like other philosophers who study the relationship between ontology and language in Aristotle,[6] observes that being precedes the categories themselves. But what is of interest to us is the recognized close relationship between being and enunciation:

> Categories are figures (skhemata) by means of which being properly speaking is expressed. ... The system of categories is the system of the ways in which being is construed. It relates the problematic of the analogy of being ... with the problematic of the metaphor in general.[7]

Rhetoric, the language of tropes and schemes, is a means of expressing being.

Contemporary theorists of character claim that characters lack being; they are functions, formal constructs, patterns, as if our pain at the death of Cordelia or pleasure at the marriage of Rosalind were simply pain or pleasure at the end of a pattern.[8] But this close relationship between *physis* and *logos*, between being and language, suggests that being is constituted for us in its expressions, and perhaps particularly, its linguistic expressions. To argue that language constitutes being is no doubt abusive, for as Cassirer suggests, language cannot precede its subject, the enunciator. Such a claim argues for a truth or universal status or ontology of language which is problematic. But in the world of poetry, in the practice of dramatic character, language in large measure constitues being, creates characters. If, as anthropologists, sociologists and psychologists claim, the self is 'a construct, the result of systems of conventions',[9] perhaps the critical gulf between characters and persons is less wide than we once imagined. In reading and watching Shakespeare's plays, in attending to the words his characters speak and to their interior dialogues, their conversations with the self, we are not only experiencing patterns, forms, and structures of plot and action, but being expressed in language.

Notes

Introduction

1 See Johnson's *Preface to Shakespeare* (1765) for the classic statement of this point of view. Johnson praises Shakespeare's characters by claiming he 'has no heroes; his scenes are occupied only by men, who act and speak as the reader thinks that he should himself have spoken or acted on the same occasion: Even where the agency is supernatural the dialogue is level with life. ... This therefore is the praise of Shakespeare, that his drama is the mirrour of life.' But Johnson also criticizes Shakespeare's conventional and unlikely plots, as in his often quoted complaint about the end of *Twelfth Night*.

2 Jonathan Culler, *Structuralist Poetics*, Ithaca, 1975, 29; for an early statement of this point of view, see Northrop Frye, 'Characterization in Shakespearean Comedy', *Shakespeare Quarterly*, 4 (1953), 271–7.

3 See Tzvetan Todorov, *Littérature et signification*, Paris, 1967, and A. J. Greimas, *Sémantique Structurale*, Paris, 1966.

4 Roland Barthes, 'Introduction à l'analyze structurale des récits', *Communications*, 8 (1966), 1–27, notes that stories in which a character in whom 'l'objet et le sujet se confondent dans un même personnage sont les récits de la quête de soi-même, de sa propre identité'. In a strikingly similar passage in his *Movements of Thought in the Nineteenth*

Century, ed. Merritt H. Moore, Chicago, 1936, rpt 1950, George H. Mead observed that 'the self belongs to the reflexive mode. One senses the self only in so far as the self assumes the role of another so that it becomes both subject and object in the same experience' (p. 63). See also Seymour Chatman's *Story and Discourse*, Ithaca, Cornell, 1978, which summarizes recent work and proposes a 'paradigm of traits' based on psychological descriptions of identity or personality.

5   In his essay, 'Character in a coherent fiction: on putting *King Lear* back together again', *Philosophy and Literature*, 7 (1983), 196–212, Sanford Freedman observes that critics agree that any discussion of character 'must start with characters' words', (p. 203).

6   See, for example, Caroline Spurgeon, *Shakespeare's Imagery*, Cambridge, 1965, orig. edn. 1935; M. M. Morozov, 'The individualization of Shakespeare's characters through imagery', *Shakespeare Survey*, 2 (1949), 83–106; Leonard Prager, 'The language of Shakespeare's low characters: an introductory study', diss. Yale, 1957; and more recently, A. R. Braunmuller, 'Characterization through language in the early plays of Shakespeare and his contemporaries', presented at the congress of the International Shakespeare Association, Stratford-upon-Avon, 1981, and Elizabeth Yearling, 'Language, theme and character in *Twelfth Night*', *Shakespeare Survey*, 34 (1981), 121–30.

7   Wolfgang Clemen, 'Shakespeare's soliloquies,' *Shakespeare's Dramatic Art*, London, 1972.

8   See, for example, Harold F. Brooks, 'Two clowns in a comedy (to say nothing of the dog): Speed, Launce (and Crab) in *The Two Gentlemen of Verona*', *Essays and Studies*, 16 (1963), 91–100.

9   For a recent and stimulating discussion of character as process, see Michael Goldman's 'Characterizing *Coriolanus*', *Shakespeare Survey*, 34 (1981), 73–84.

10   Clemen, *English Tragedy Before Shakespeare*, trans. T. S. Dorsch, London, 1955, 12.

11   See William N. Dodd, 'Metalanguage and character in drama', *Lingua e stile*, 14 (1979), who observes that the 'absence of an onstage fictive receiver gives prominence to the external receiver, the spectator', (p. 147).

12   Dodd, cited above, argues that 'what critics sometimes describe as "psychology" is actually ... a semiological phenomenon, namely internal metalanguage', (p. 145); see also Jirí Vel-

truský's discussion of character in *Drama as Literature*, Lisse, 1977.

13 Édouard Dujardin, one of the earliest practitioners of the interior monologue and certainly its earliest theoretician, pointedly links the device to drama. He dedicates his *Monologue Interieur* to Racine whom he regards as the supreme artist of the inner life because of his success at representing the subconscious. See also Robert Scholes and Robert Kellogg, *The Nature of Narrative*, New York, 1966, 180–5. Scholes and Kellogg distinguish between stream of consciousness, which they argue is organized on 'psychologically oriented patterns', and interior monologue, which uses dialogue and has traditionally 'invited rhetorical display'. But Dorrit Cohn's analysis of the formal elements of both stream of consciousness and interior monologue suggests that no clear distinction can be made between 'psychologically oriented' and rhetorically organized patterns; see *Transparent Minds: Narrative Modes for Presenting Consciousness in Fiction*, Princeton, 1978, 90. See also Jan Mukařovský's discussion of dialogue in *The Word and Verbal Art*, ed. and trans. John Burbank and Peter Steiner, New Haven, 1977, esp. 81–115; M. M. Bakhtin, *The Dialogic Imagination*, trans. Caryl Emerson and Michael Holquist, Austin, 1981, 84–258; and L. S. Vygotsky's work on the internalized thinking aloud of children, which suggests that dialogue may indeed be a feature of mental process, not simply a rhetorical means for representing it.

14 For a description of the essential aspects of dialogue, see Mukařovský, *The Word and Verbal Art*, pp. 81–115; Bennison Gray, 'From discourse to "dialog",' *Journal of Pragmatics*, 3 (1977), 283–97; and Udo Fries, 'Topics and problems in "dialogue linguistics"', *Studia Anglica Posaniensia*, 7 (1975), 7–15; I distinguish dialogue from conversation and its linguistic description in the work of Paul Grice, 'Logic and conversation', *Syntax and Semantics*, eds Peter Cole and Jerry L. Morgan, New York, 1975, III, 41–58.

15 The influence of the Psychomachia and its more flexible counterpart, the spiritual journey, should not be underestimated in any consideration of the inner debate in soliloquy as a strategy of character development; see Edgar T. Schell, 'On the imitation of life's pilgrimage in *The Castle of Perseverence*', *Medieval English Drama*, eds Jerome Taylor and Alan H. Nelson, Chicago, 1972, 279–91.

16　Leo Salingar, *Shakespeare and the Traditions of Comedy*, London, 1974, 222.

17　See, for example, Harriett Hawkins, 'The Devil's party: virtues and vices in *Measure for Measure*', *Shakespeare Survey*, 31 (1978), 105–13.

18　See A. D. Nuttall's brief discussion of the lifelike in Shakespeare in his 'Realistic convention and conventional realism in Shakespeare', *Shakespeare Survey*, 34 (1981), 33–7.

19　E. H. Gombrich, *Art and Illusion*, Princeton, 1960, rpt 1972, 8.

1　*The inward springs:* Measure for Measure *II, ii, 162–87*

1　W. H. Auden, 'The Globe', *The Dyer's Hand and Other Essays*, London, 1948, rpt 1962, 175.

2　If our theatrical experience does not convince us that *Measure for Measure* is a comedy, we should remember that it was one of the first of Shakespeare's plays to be revived during the Restoration. In his production (1661–2), Davenant suppressed a great deal of the play's bawdry by combining *Measure for Measure* with the Beatrice and Benedick plot from *Much Ado*, a marriage which emphasizes the play's comic features; see also Roger Sale's 'The comic mode of *Measure for Measure*', *Shakespeare Quarterly*, 19 (1968), 55–61.

3　References to *Measure for Measure* are to the Arden edition ed. J. W. Lever, London, 1965; rpt New York, 1967; for a review of the criticism of Angelo's character, see Rosalind Miles, *The Problem of Measure for Measure*, London, 1976.

4　See George H. Mead, *Movements of Thought in the Nineteenth Century*, ed. Merritt H. Moore, Chicago, 1936, rpt 1950, who defines thinking as 'a process of conversation with one's self when the individual takes the attitude of the other, especially when he takes the common attitude of the whole group' (p. 380).

5　Roger Fowler's account of the formal elements which construct the relationship among implied author, narrator and implied reader in 'The referential code and narrative authority', *Language and Style*, 3 (1977), 129–61, though limited to narrative, nevertheless is suggestive for drama as well.

6　Dorritt Cohn, *Transparent Minds: Narrative Modes for Presenting Consciousness in Fiction*, Princeton, 1978, 90.

7　See William Empson's excellent essay, 'Sense in *Measure for Measure*', *The Structure of Complex Words*, London, 1951; for a summary of the glosses on these lines and Angelo's soliloquy, see *A New Variorum Edition of Shakespeare: Measure for Measure*, ed. Mark Eccles, New York, 1980, 95 ff.

8   Jan Mukarovský, *The Word and Verbal Art*, ed. and trans. John Burbank and Peter Steiner, New Haven, 1977, 60.

9   For a persuasive if sympathetic argument on behalf of Angelo's character and his development, see W. M. T. Dodd's 'The character of Angelo in *Measure for Measure*', *Modern Language Review*, 41 (1946), 246–55; Malheureux's speech in John Marston's *The Dutch Courtesan*, first staged in 1604, though much less subtle, contains many of the same features – the broken rhythms and self-address – which we find in Angelo's soliloquy. Miles, in *The Problem of Measure for Measure*, considers Malheureux almost the only contemporary character to resemble Angelo in plight and dramatic treatment, pp. 200–4.

10   For a more detailed account of the grammar school curriculum, see T. W. Baldwin, *William Shakespeare's Small Latine and Lesse Greeke*, Urbana, 1944; Virgil K. Whitaker, *Shakespeare's Use of Learning*, San Marino, 1953, and Charles O. McDonald's *The Rhetoric of Tragedy*, Amherst, 1966, 75–92, who discusses Tudor rhetorical training; see also his chapter on Seneca in which he notes the use of rhetorical questions and self-address in the tragic soliloquy, pp. 55–68.

11   Donald K. Clark documents the popularity of Aphthonius in 'The rise and fall of *Progymnasmata* in sixteenth and seventeenth century grammar schools', *Speech Monographs*, 19 (1952), 259–63; for a translation of the Greek original, see Raymond E. Nadeau's 'The *Progymnasmata* of Aphthonius in translation', *Speech Monographs*, 19 (1952), 264–85.

12   Wesley Trimpi, 'The ancient hypothesis of fiction: an essay on the origins of literary theory', *Traditio*, 27 (1971), 12.

13   For an excellent discussion of place logic and its generative possibilities, see Marion Trousdale, *Shakespeare and the Rhetoricians*, Chapel Hill, NC, 1982.

14   E. H. Kantorowicz, 'The sovereignty of the artist: a note on legal maxims and Renaissance theories of art', *Selected Studies*, New York, 1965, 352–65; see also Sidney's *Apology for Poetry*, 'And doth the Lawyer lye ...', pp. 185–6.

15   My discussion of *qualitas* draws in part on Wesley Trimpi's essay, 'The quality of fiction: the rhetorical transmission of literary theory', *Traditio*, 30 (1974), 1–118; see also Trousdale's discussion of the role of ornament and its effect on reader and

viewer in *Shakespeare and the Rhetoricians*, 81–94, and her final chapter on the didactic element in Renaissance drama, 114–59.

16 Trimpi, 'Quality of fiction', 12; Giorgio Melchiori has recently defined rhetoric as the '*art* of creating consensus through linguistic communication and not simply (as is generally assumed) a classification of the forms of merely verbal expression into figures, tropes and schemata', 'The rhetoric of character construction: *Othello*', *Shakespeare Survey*, 34 (1981), 61–72.

17 See particularly M. C. Bradbrook, 'Authority, truth and justice in *Measure for Measure*' in Robert Ornstein, ed. *Discussion of Shakespeare's Problem Comedies*, Boston, 1961.

18 Joel Altman, *The Tudor Play of the Mind*, Berkeley, 1978.

2   *Comic plot conventions in* Measure for Measure

1   Roland Barthes, 'L'effet de réel', *Communications*, 11 (1968), 84–9.

2   See Gregory Bateson, 'Conventions of communication', in *Communication: The Social Matrix of Psychiatry*, eds Jurgen Ruesch and Gregory Bateson, New York, 1968, 212.

3   See, for example, Martin Price, 'The other self: thoughts about character in the novel', *Imagined Worlds: Essays ... in Honour of John Butt*, ed. M. Mack, London, 1968, 279–99; Roland Barthes, *S/Z*, Paris, 1970; and Jonathan Culler, *Flaubert: The Uses of Uncertainty*, London, 1974.

4   In addition to the studies by Stevenson, Gless, Leonard and Miles cited below, see also Harriett Hawkins *Likenesses of Truth* and her article 'The Devil's party: virtues and vices in *Measure for Measure*', *Shakespeare Survey*, 31 (1978), 105–13 and Meredith Skura, 'New interpretations for interpretation in *Measure for Measure*', *Boundaries*, II (1980), 39–59.

5   For the notion of convention as contract and for a brief history of literary convention, see Harry Levin, 'Notes on convention', *Perspectives of Criticism, Harvard Studies in Comparative Literature*, 20 (1960), 55–83.

6   See Darryl J. Gless, *Measure for Measure, the Law and the Convent*, Princeton, 1979, for scriptural parallels and a discussion of contemporary religious materials and their relevance to genre and character.

7   For a more detailed discussion of substitution in *Measure for*

Measure, see Robert Ornstein, 'The human comedy in *Measure for Measure*', *University of Kansas City Review*, 24 (1957), 15–22, and more recently Nancy Leonard, 'Substitution in Shakespeare's problem comedies', *English Literary Renaissance*, 9 (1979), 281–301.

8 Ernest Schanzer points out the pun in Angelo's name on the ten-shilling gold coin known as the angel in *The Problem Plays of Shakespeare*, London, 1963, 94.

9 The Duke's role in the action has been much debated. Clifford Leech, 'The meaning of *Measure for Measure*', *Shakespeare Survey*, 3 (1950), 69–70, finds the Duke inconsistent and damnable; Harold S. Wilson, 'Action and symbol in *Measure for Measure* and *The Tempest*', *Shakespeare Quarterly*, 4 (1953), 379 and Schanzer, *Problem Plays*, 113–17, both find the Duke's actions defensible and necessary; Mary Lascelles, *Shakespeare's Measure for Measure*, Folcroft, Pa, 1953, gives the historical, literary and folklore background for the motif of the disguised ruler as justification for his role in the action. Recently Leonard Tenenhouse has pointed out that there were numerous 'disguised ruler plays' written and produced around the same time, 'Representing power: *Measure for Measure* in its time', *Genre*, 15 (1982), 139–56. Rosalind Miles surveys the critical problems traditionally associated with the Duke's character in *The Problem of Measure for Measure*, London, 1976; for a cogent argument on behalf of the Duke and the play's unity, see Louise Schleiner, 'Providential improvisation in *Measure for Measure*, *PMLA* 97 (1982), 227–36. Richard A. Levin, 'Duke Vincentio and Angelo: would "a feather turn the scale"?' *Studies in English Literature* 22 (1982), argues that the Duke need not be explained in terms of convention, but rather as a character who succumbs to temptation.

10 Kenneth Muir, *Shakespeare's Sources*, London, 1957, rpt 1961, I, 8.

11 Lever, ed. *Measure for Measure*, 46, and J. V. Cunningham, 'Essence in "The Phoenix and the Turtle"', *English Literary History*, 19 (1952), 266.

12 Cf. chapter 1, p. 133, n. 7; in his introduction to the 1977 volume of *English Institute Essays* devoted to *Psychoanalysis and the Question of the Text*, Geoffrey Hartman notes that in contemporary psychoanalytic theory 'the concept of identity in the ethical or psychological realm has been linked to the problem of reference in the linguistic realm', p. xi.

13 See chapter 1.

14 Many critics have noted the similarity between Angelo and Isabella. See, for example, Schanzer, *Problem Plays*, p. 94, who compares Isabella's Pharisaical view of divine law with Angelo's view of man-made law. Schanzer argues that even Isabella's forgiveness of Angelo at the end of the play is legalistic rather than personal, Christian forgiveness. D. L. Stevenson in his book, *The Achievement of Measure for Measure*, Ithaca, 1966, disputes this view. He claims 'she is a kind of obverse of Angelo ... the play is allowed to come to an end only at the moment of exact equivalence between Isabella and Angelo. It ends only when Isabella has really become the thing she argued for in Act II, that is, merciful ("against all sense," as the Duke points out)' (p. 44).

15 L. C. Knights' 'The ambiguity of *Measure for Measure*', *Scrutiny*, 10 (1942), 222.

16 René Girard's *Violence et le Sacré*, Paris, 1972, is suggestive and useful to an interpretation of *Measure for Measure*, particularly the final act. Girard argues that all desire is mimetic and therefore generates a crisis of difference between father and son, brother and brother, man and his neighbor. Such contention leads to reciprocal violence which can only be arrested by collective aggression against a surrogate victim. Only through such ritual violence, whether enacted by the community at large, as in primitive societies, or by its representative, as in the judicial system of modern culture, can such violence be contained, difference re-inscribed, and order maintained.

17 David K. Lewis, *Convention: A Philosophical Study*, Cambridge, 1969, 19. For a concise introduction and bibliography on convention, see Lawrence Manley, *Convention 1500–1750*, Cambridge, 1980, 1–14.

18 In his discussion of *Twelfth Night*, Porter Williams argues generally that mistakes in identity are not superficial plot devices, but reveal subconscious patterns of human behaviour 'Mistakes in *Twelfth Night* and their resolution: a study in some relationships of plot and theme,' *PMLA*, 6 (1961), 193–9. For an interesting discussion of Shakespeare's use of comic conventions including mistaken identity in the tragedies, see Susan Snyder, *The Comic Matrix of Shakespeare's Tragedies*, Princeton, 1980, and Robert R. Hellenga, 'Elizabethan dramatic conventions and Elizabethan reality', *Renaissance Drama*, 12 (1981), 27–49.

3 *Menander and New Comedy*

1 Bernard Knox, 'The Tempest and comic tradition', *English Stage Comedy*, ed. W. K. Wimsatt, Jr, *English Institute Essays*, 1954, New York, 1955, 52–73.

2 The Letters of Ausonius, trans. O. M. Dalton, Oxford, 1915, II, 24.

3 Stephen Gosson in his *Plays Confuted*, London, 1582, D5ᵛ, cites *Amadis*, Heliodorus' *Aethiopian History* and the Arthurian tales as major sources for contemporary drama; Louis B. Wright documents the popular taste for romances in his *Middle Class Culture in Elizabethan England*, Chapel Hill, 1935, chs 4, 11; for the influence of hellenistic romance in the Renaissance and on Shakespeare, see Samuel L. Wolff, *The Greek Romances in Elizabethan Prose*, New York, 1912, and Carol Gesner, *Shakespeare and the Greek Romance*, Lexington, Kentucky, 1970. Bernard Knox discusses the relation between Euripides and New Comedy, 'Euripidean comedy', *The Rarer Action*, edsAlan Cheuse and Richard Koffler, New Brunswick, NJ, 1970, 68–96; see also Sander M. Goldberg, *The Making of Menander's Comedy*, Berkeley, 1980, and Madeleine Doran's discussion of Renaissance habits of reading and illustrating Roman comedy as romance in *Endeavors of Art*, 3rd edn, 1954, rpt Madison, 1972, 174–5. There is evidence that this narrative mode of reading and illustrating derives from early fifth-century manuscripts of Terence: Leslie Webber Jones and C. R. Morey, *The Miniatures of the Manuscripts of Terence*, Princeton, 1931, 205 ff.

4 For an interesting discussion of subtle variations in type characterization, see W. Thomas MacCary, 'Menander's characters: their names, roles and masks', *Transactions and Proceedings of the American Philological Association*, 101 (1970), 277–98.

5 Leo Salingar, *Shakespeare and the Traditions of Comedy*, London, 1974, 126.

6 See E. Frankel, *Plautinisches in Plautus*, Berlin, 1922; M. Tierney, 'Aristotle and Menander', *Proceedings of the Royal Irish Academy*, 43 (1936), 241–54; A. W. Gomme, 'Menander', *Essays in Greek History and Literature*, Oxford, 1937, 249–95; L. A. Post, *From Homer to Menander: Forces in Greek Poetic Fiction*, Berkeley, 1951, 233–4; F. H. Sandbach, *Ancient Culture and Society: The Comic Theatre of Greece and Rome*,

London, 1977, 102; and most recently Goldberg, *The Making of Menander's Comedy*.

7   See R. Schottlaender, 'Menanders *Dyskolos* und der Zusammenbruch der "Autarkie"', *Schriften Akademie Berlin*, 50 (1965), 33–42, cited in Thomas G. Rosenmeyer, *The Green Cabinet*, Berkeley, University of California Press, 1969, 105.

8   F. H. Sandbach and A. W. Gomme argue that though this device was sometimes used parodically in Old Comedy, there could 'be no question of parody here; the scene which begins here has a colour less comic than that of any other part of the play', *Menander, A Commentary*, Oxford 1973, 239–40; for general studies of the monologue in Menander, see Leo Freidrich, *Der Monolog im Drama*, Berlin 1908; John Dean Bickford, 'Soliloquy in ancient comedy', diss. Princeton, 1922, and John Blundell, *Menander and the Monologue*, Gottingen, 1980.

9   *Menandri Reliquiae Selectae*, ed. F. H. Sandbach, Oxford, 1972, rpt 1976, 712–32; translations by R. Goodwin.

10 ΕΠΙΤΡΕΠΟΝΤΕΣ, lines 894–9, *Menandri Reliquiae Selectae*.

11 ΕΠΙΤΡΕΠΟΝΤΕΣ, lines 908–32, *Menandri Reliquiae Selectae*; I have followed Wilamowitz and Körte, who make the Power speak from line 912, rather than Gomme and Sandbach's punctuation here.

12 David Bain, *Actors and Audience: A Study of Asides and Related Conventions in Greek Drama*, Oxford, 1977, 148.

13 Robert Weimann, *Shakespeare und die Tradition des Volkstheaters, Soziologie, Dramaturgie, Gestaltung*, 1967, trans. as *Shakespeare and the Popular Tradition in the Theatre*, ed. Robert Schwarz, Baltimore, 1978, 9.

14 ΕΠΙΤΡΕΠΟΝΤΕΣ, l. 912; Gomme and Sandbach, *Menandri Reliquiae Selectae*, p. 364.

15 E. W. Handley, 'The conventions of the comic stage and their exploitation by Menander', *Ménandre*, Genève, 1969, 21; see also Goldberg's interesting discussion of Menander's mixture of what he calls tragic and comic modes in *The Making of Menander's Comedy*, pp. 29 ff.

16 Wolfgang Clemen, *Shakespeare's Dramatic Art*, London, 1972, notes that Shakespeare uses all of the classical traditions of what Clemen terms apostrophe in finding imagined partners for his soliloquizing characters (p. 156); see also E. G. Turner, 'The rhetoric of question and answer in Menander', *Drama and Mimesis, Themes in Drama*, 2 (Cambridge, 1980), 1–24.

17   Weimann, *Shakespeare and the Popular Tradition*, pp. 8–9.

18   ibid., p. 9.

19   T. B. L. Webster, *An Introduction to Menander*, Manchester, 1974, 91.

20   Post, *Greek Poetic Fiction*, p. 316.

4   *Plautus and Terence*

1   Richard Hosley, 'The formal influence of Plautus and Terence', *Elizabethan Theatre, Stratford-upon-Avon Studies*, 9 (1966), argues for the importance of Plautus over Terence in the Renaissance.

2   See, for example, Hazel E. Barnes, 'The case of Sosia versus Sosia', *Classical Journal*, 53 (1957–8), 19.

3   English translations are from *The Rope and Other Plays*, trans. E. F. Watling, New York, 1964, rpt 1977.

4   *Jack Juggler, Malone Society Reprints*, eds Benjamin Evans and W. W. Greg, 3rd edn, London, 1937.

5   See John Wright's excellent essay 'The transformations of Pseudolus', *Transactions and Proceedings of the American Philological Association*, 105 (1975).

6   All translations are from *The Pot of Gold and Other Plays*, trans. E. F. Watling, New York, 1977.

7   *Commentum Terenti*, Lipsiae, 1905, II, 184.

8   See Edwin W. Robbins, *Dramatic Characterization in Printed Commentaries of Terence, 1473–1600, Illinois Studies in Language and Literature*, 35 (4), 107 ff.

9   Evanthius, 'De Fabula' IV, 2, *Commentum Terenti*, I, 21.

10   Jodocus Badius Ascensius, *Praenotamenta Ascensiana*, 1502.

11   For the classic statement on types and decorum, see Madeleine Doran, *Endeavors of Art*, 3rd edn, 1954, rpt Madison, 1972, 218 ff.

12   G. B. Giraldi Cintio is one among many Renaissance critics who take up Donatus' point about individualizing types; he cites contemporary plays such as Ariosto's *Cassaria* as well as the standard Terentian examples. 'Discorso ... intorno al Comporre delle Comedie', 1543, *Discorsi*, Venice, 1554, 214–15.

13   All references in Latin are to the *Oxford Classical Text* edition of Terence, eds Robert Kaner and Wallace M. Lindsay. English translations are from Frank O. Copley, *The Comedies of Terence*, Indianapolis, IN, 1976, 123.

14   See Robbins, *Dramatic Characterization*, who notes that though the courtesan is not made to suffer much ridicule at the

hands of the dramatist, her generic evil is fully emphasized by the sixteenth-century commentators, p. 85.

5   *The enchantments of Circe*

1   See David Orr's presentation of the statistical evidence in *Italian Renaissance Drama in England before 1625, University of North Carolina Studies in Comparative Literature*, 40, Chapel Hill, 1970.

2   Albert Feuillerat, *Documents Relating to the Office of Revels in the Time of Queen Elizabeth*, London, 1903, 225 ff. and *Acts of Privy Council*, II, 88.

3   Consider, for example, Marston's knowledge of Italy in his words 'To the Reader' which precede *The Malcontent*, or the propensity of Elizabethan playwrights to Italianize their plays as in *Romeo and Juliet*, in which the Latin ending of Romeus' name from Arthur Brooke's poem becomes Romeo.

4   Stephen Gosson, *The Schoole of Abuse*, B5^r, facsimile ed. rpt *The English Experience*, 523, Amsterdam, 1972.

5   Madeleine Doran, for example, in her *Endeavors of Art: A Study of Form in Elizabethan Drama*, 1954, rpt Madison, 1972, considers Italian comedy as only a branch of Roman comedy.

6   G. K. Hunter, 'Italian tragicomedy on the English stage', *Renaissance Drama*, 6 (1973), 123–48.

7   See J. W. Lever's introduction to the Arden edition of *Measure for Measure*, London, 1965, and Arthur Kirsch, *Jacobean Dramatic Perspectives*, Charlottesville, Va, 1972.

8   L. G. Clubb, 'Woman as Wonder, generic figure in Italian and Shakespearean comedy', *Studies in the Continental Background of Renaissance English Literature*, eds Dale B. J. Randall and G. W. Williams, Durham, NC, 1977, 109–32.

9   L. G. Clubb, 'Italian comedy and the *Comedy of Errors*', *Comparative Literature*, 19 (1967), 244–5.

10 Leo Salingar, *Shakespeare and the Traditions of Comedy*, London, 1974, 222.

11 ibid., p. 217.

12 Salingar, 'The design of *Twelfth Night*', *Shakespeare Quarterly*, 9 (1958), 122.

13 Italian dramatists took their heroines, young women who disguise themselves, suffer and finally win their beloveds, from medieval romance and *novelle*.

14 Quoted in Salingar, *Traditions*, p. 194; for Garzoni's probable source, see *Il Cortegiano*, II, 11.

15 The Intronati, *La commedia degl'Ingannati*, ed. Florindo Cerreta, Firenze, Olschki, 1980, 151. All references are to this edition.

16 *The Deceived, Five Italian Renaissance Comedies*, ed. and trans. Bruce Penman, New York, 1978, 216. All references are to this edition.

17 In his discussion of inner speech in children, L. S. Vygotsky remarks upon three features, all characteristic of Lelia's soliloquy: preservation of the predicate despite abbreviation; syntactic impoverishment; a corresponding semantic enrichment; *Thought and Language*, ed. and trans. Gertrude Vakar, Cambridge, 1962.

18 Penman's choice of 'lucky' to translate 'beato' and 'felice' is unfortunate; 'blessed' and 'happy' would better communicate the force of Flamminio's exclamation.

19 The Italian might be better translated, 'Pardon me, if what I have done displeases you whom I didn't know, because I am most repentant and realize my fault.'

20 Salingar calls it 'the first modern comedy in which characters are shown to follow a credible purpose, see the consequences of their actions, waver, develop and change', *Traditions*, p. 217.

21 In his 'Politics and comedy in the early years of the Accademia degli Intronati of Siena', Nerida Newbigin points out that Balía records suggest the play had been in preparation much longer, *Il teatro italiano de Rinascimento*, *Milano*, 1980, 131.

22 See Mario Baratto's excellent discussion of Italian Renaissance comedy and society in *La Commedia del Cinquecento*, Vicenza, 1975.

23 Lodovico Castelvetro, *Poetica*, Basel, 1576, 61, quoted in Salingar, *Traditions*, p. 185.

24 Salingar, 'Design of *Twelfth Night*, p. 122.

25 Because Salingar limits his argument to *I Suppositi, La Calandria*, and *Gl'Ingannati*, all three written and performed before 1537, he misses the crucial relationship between late *commedia grave* and Shakespearean comedy. See Lever, ed. *Measure for Measure*; Kirsch, *Jacobean Dramatic Perspectives*; and Clubb, 'Italian Comedy'.

26 See Guido Baldi, 'Le commedie di Sforza Oddi e l'ideologia della controriforma', *Lettere Italiane*, 23 (1971), 42–62.

27 Boccaccio's tale of Gillette of Narbonne, III, 9, certainly a

source for *All's Well that Ends Well*, may also have provided a model for Bargagli's Drusilla; see also *Decameron*, IV, 8, for another possible analogue.

28 In Borsellino's collection, based on the 1606 and 1611 editions, Drusilla is a native of Lyon. The Fench setting reflects changes made after Bargagli's death by his brother Scipione for the first production in 1589 at the marriage of Ferdinand de' Medici to Christine of Lorraine. The Gallic locale served to compliment the new French duchess.

29 Girolamo Bargagli, *La Pellegrina*, ed. Florindo Cerreta, Firenze, 1971, 86. All references are to this edition.

30 Drusilla's refusal even of a kiss before a public betrothal reflects the stricter marriage laws which resulted from the Council of Trent.

31 See Baratto's discussion of comic polarities, *La Commedia del Cinquecento*, pp. 72 ff.

32 Clubb, 'Woman as Wonder', pp. 109–32.

33 Salingar, 'Design of *Twelfth Night*', p. 222.

6 *'And all their minds transfigur'd': Shakespeare's early comedies*

1 Bernard Knox, '*The Tempest* and the ancient comic tradition', *English Institute Essays*, 1954, 54.

2 Harry Levin, 'Two comedies of errors', *Stratford Papers on Shakespeare*, ed. B. W. Jackson, Toronto, 1964, 43.

3 All references are to the Arden edition of *The Comedy of Errors*, ed. R. A. Foakes, London, 1962, rpt 1969.

4 See particularly Harold Brooks, 'Themes and structure in *The Comedy of Errors*', *Early Shakespeare, Shakespeare Institute Studies*, eds J. R. Brown and Bernard Harris, London, 1961, rpt 1966, 55–72.

5 For the notion of 'losing to find' in Shakespearean comedy, see Leo Salingar, *Shakespeare and the Traditions of Comedy*, London, 1974, 25, and Alexander Leggatt, *Shakespeare's Comedy of Love*, London, 1974, 166.

6 G. K. Hunter's *John Lyly, the Humanist as Courtier*, Cambridge, 1962, discusses Shakespearean metamorphosis which threatens our assured sense of personal identity. For the intellectual and literary history of this line in *Errors*, see T. W. Baldwin's lengthy chapter in *On the Compositional Genetics of the Comedy of Errors*, Urbana, 1965.

7 Language of change and transformation pervades the play. See I, ii, 95 ff.; II, ii, 8, 168, 194–5; III, i, 34; III, ii, 29 ff., 142 ff.; IV, iii, 10–11, 38; V, i, 308 ff.

8 Coincidentally, it was Menander who, along with St Paul, established Ephesus' reputation as a city of sorcery and cozenage.

9 The *Oxford English Dictionary* defines *confound* as 'to defeat utterly, to spoil or corrupt; to throw into confusion of mind, feelings; to mix up or mingle so that elements become difficult to distinguish; and to mix up an idea, erroneously treat as identical', all meanings which bear on Shakespeare's use of the word here. There are examples from the period for all definitions.

10 See Derek Traversi, *An Approach to Shakespeare*, London, 1938, rpt 1968, I, 78 ff. for an interesting discussion of Antipholus' language. Words such as *dote*, *siren*, *mermaid* and the like seriously undermine a wholly positive interpretation of the twin's love at this point.

11 For an interesting discussion of this issue in Shakespeare, see Robert Weimann, 'Society and the individual in Shakespeare's conception of character', *Shakespeare Survey*, 34 (1981), 23–31.

12 The text insists on union of the protagonist with a woman in marriage and therefore does not support W. Thomas Mac-Cary's reading in '*The Comedy of Errors:* A different kind of comedy', *New Literary History*, 9 (1978), in which he argues *Errors* is a narcissistic comedy in which Antipholus overcomes pre-Oedipal fears of his mother.

13 G. K. Hunter, *Shakespeare: The Late Comedies*, London, 1959, 17.

14 For a dissenting view, see Joan Stansbury, 'Characterization of the young lovers in *A Midsummer Night's Dream*', *Shakespeare Survey*, 35 (1982), 57–63.

15 Most readers agree with C. L. Barber who observes in his *Shakespeare's Festive Comedy*, Princeton, 1959, that 'the comedy's irony about love's motives and choices expresses love's power not as an attribute of personality but as an impersonal force beyond the persons concerned', (p. 130).

16 See Harold F. Brooks' commentary on Bottom's soliloquy in the Arden edition, London, 1979, cxvii; all references are to this edition.

17   See Walter Cohen's discussion of the clown's function in his fine essay, '*The Merchant of Venice* and the possibilities of historical criticism', *ELH*, 49, (1983), esp. 779–81, and Robert Weimann's *Shakespeare and the Popular Tradition in the Theatre*, Baltimore, 1978, esp. 39–48, 120–50.

18   All references are to the Arden edition of *Love's Labour's Lost*, ed. Richard David, London, 1956, rpt 1965.

19   See Weimann, 'Society and the individual'.

20   *Clyomon and Clamydes*, ed. Betty J. Littleton, The Hague, 1968, 109–10.

21   The Arden edition of *The Two Gentlemen of Verona*, ed. Clifford Leech, London, 1969.

22   H. J. Neushäfer, *Boccaccio und der Beginn der Novelle*, München, 1969, 45, cited by Karlheinz Stierle, 'L'histoire comme exemple, l'exemple comme histoire', *Poétique*, 10 (1972), 176–98.

7   *Magic versus time:* As You Like It *and* Twelfth Night

1   For a dissenting view see Thomas Kelly, 'Shakespeare's romantic heroes: Orlando reconsidered', *Shakespeare Quarterly*, 24 (1973), who defends Orlando against the usual claim that he is tested and educated by Rosalind. Kelly argues that Orlando is as much a role-player as Rosalind herself, pp. 72 ff.

2   For the classic statements of *As You Like It* as a play of testing and education, see Helen Gardner, '*As You Like It*', *More Talking of Shakespeare*, ed. John Garrett, London, 1969, and H. B. Charlton, *Shakespearean Comedy*, London, 1966.

3   Critics have made only general remarks about Rosalind's education or development, cf. David Young, *The Heart's Forest*, New Haven, 1972, who observes that 'her disguise is a means of revelation allowing her to avoid constraining roles'.

4   All references are the Arden edition of *As You Like It*, ed. Agnes Latham, London, 1975.

5   D. J. Palmer in his essay 'Art and nature in *As You Like It*', *Philological Quarterly*, 49 (1970), 36, suggests that through the 'almost operatic artifice of this quartet each finds his own image in Silvius's idealized picture'. He also notes the formal rhetoric given to the reciprocity of the lovers' plight.

6   See Albert R. Cirillo, '*As You Like It:* pastoralism gone awry', *English Literary History*, 38 (1971), 19–39.

7   See, for example, Karen Greif, 'Play and playing in *Twelfth Night*', *Shakespeare Survey*, 34 (1981), 121–30.

8   All references are to the Arden edition of *Twelfth Night*, eds J. M. Lothian and T. W. Craik, London, 1975, rpt 1978.

9   I accept the First Folio reading of this line: 'worne', in the sense of 'worn out, impaired by use, spent', or even perhaps 'hackneyed', is perfectly in keeping with Orsino's description of men's fancies. The Second Folio reading, 'won', though arguably idiomatic, is after all an unnecessary and even clichéd emendation.

10 For an interesting discussion of Feste's role in the action, see Alan S. Downer's essay 'Feste's night', *College English*, 13 (1952), 258–65.

11 For an interesting discussion of 'mirroring' in the comedies, see Jorg Hasler, *Shakespeare's Theatrical Notation: The Comedies*, Berne, 1974.

12 E. M. W. Tillyard, *Shakespeare's Problem Plays*, London, 1957, 97. See also Clifford Leech's critique from essentially the same perspective in *'Twelfth Night* or what delights you', *Twentieth Century Interpretations of Twelfth Night*, ed. Walter N. King, Englewood Cliffs, 1968, 72.

13 Both Sidney and Jonson, as well as many lesser Renaissance theorists, base the analogy between the verbal and visual arts on the imitation of inner nature rather than outward appearance. See O. B. Hardison, *English Literary Criticism: The Renaissance*, New York, 1963, for references from Jonson, pp. 274–5; Wilson, *Action and Symbol*, p. 69; Ascham, *The Scholemaster*, p. 61; and Puttenham, p. 175; for references in Sidney, see Geoffrey Shepherd's edition, London, 1965, 51, 102, 107.

14 See Richard Henze, *'Twelfth Night:* free disposition on the sea of love', *Sewanee Review*, 83 (1975), 267–83, for an interpretation of the play based on the oppositions of giving and taking, particularly Sebastian's hazard of self.

15 Nancy K. Hayles, 'Sexual disguise in *As You Like It* and *Twelfth Night*', *Shakespeare Survey*, 33 (1979), 63–73, distinguishes between sexual disguise which explores sexual role-playing, power and control (*AYLI*) and that which considers the metaphysical implications of disguise and appearance versus essence (*TN*).

16 Cf. Julian Markels, *'Twelfth Night* and *King Lear*', *Shakespeare Quarterly*, 15 (1964), 75–88, who claims that the steward's 'clarity of mind' and 'correctness of his philosophic manners', and 'his ability to participate suavely with the Fool in just the same sort of

catechism by which we have already seen the fool mend Olivia', prove that he has developed and learned from his errors.

8   *Mistaking in* Much Ado

1   J. R. Mulryne, *Shakespeare: Much Ado About Nothing*, Arnold *Studies in English Literature*, 16, London, 1965, 18.

2   E. M. W. Tillyard, *Shakespeare's Problem Comedies*, London, 1969, 134; see also Kenneth Muir, *Shakespeare's Sources*, London, 1957, rpt 1961, I, 181, who claims that in IV–V, 'theatrical intrigue takes the place of psychological profundity and great poetry'.

3   Jean Howard, '*Measure for Measure* and the restraints of convention', *Essays in Literature*, 10, (1983), p. 148–58, see also George E. Rowe Jr's introduction to *Thomas Middleton and the New Comedy Tradition*, Lincoln, 1979, in which he discusses how Renaissance playwrights, especially Middleton, question 'the assumptions and values which underlie the form and conventions of New Comedy', (p. 9).

4   Cf. E. C. Pettet, *Shakespeare and the Romance Tradition*, London, 1949, 124; Charles T. Prouty, *The Sources of Much Ado About Nothing: A Critical Study*, New Haven, 1950, 43; James Smith, '*Much Ado About Nothing:* notes from a book in progress', *Scrutiny*, 13 (1963); and Walter N. King, 'Much ado about something', *Shakespeare Quarterly*, 15 (1964), 150.

5   Though Claudio's detractors have been more numerous than his supporters, see T. W. Craik, '*Much Ado About Nothing*', *Scrutiny*, 19 (1953), 299, for a defense of his character.

6   All references are to the Arden edition, ed. A. R. Humphreys, London, 1981.

7   John Anson, 'Dramatic convention in Shakespeare's middle comedies', diss. Berkeley, 1964, 151.

8   E. K. Chambers, *Shakespeare: A Survey*, Oxford, 1925, p. 134; for the historical argument see Prouty, *Sources*, p. 46, and Nadine Page, 'The public repudiation of Hero', *PMLA*, 50 (1935), 743 ff.; J. K. Neill proposes perhaps the most audacious defense of Claudio in 'More ado about Claudio: an acquittal for the slandered groom', *Shakespeare Quarterly*, 3 (1952), 91–107.

9   Elliot Krieger points out Claudio's 'mechanistic refusal to question convention', and does not see even his denunciation as exceptional in the presentation of the count's character, 'Social

relations and the social order in *Much Ado'*, *Shakespeare Survey*, 32 (1979), 49–61.

10 Jorg Hasler, *Shakespeare's Theatrical Notation: The Comedies*, Bern, 1974, 70; his discussion of how Claudio changes in this scene is instructive.

11 Shakespeare also employs the rhetoric of consciousness in Leonato's monologue in IV, i, 120 ff. The rhetorical questions, broken lines, and complicated syntax reveal the depth of his emotion. The reiteration of the first person possessive pronoun suggests the problematic nature of Leonato's relationship with his daughter. Both he and Claudio seek to possess Hero; when her identity as chaste and dutiful daughter is jeopardized their respective identities as father and courtly lover are threatened as well. In the play world loss of maidenhead signals loss of identity.

12 Hasler, *Shakespeare's Theatrical Notation*, p. 71.

13 See Anson's discussion of Benedick's relation to the Plautine *miles*, 'Dramatic Convention', p. 137.

14 M. C. Bradbrook, *Shakespeare and Elizabethan Poetry*, London, 1952, 187.

15 Hasler, *Shakespeare's Theatrical Notation*, p. 72.

16 See R. G. Hunter, *Shakespeare and the Comedy of Forgiveness*, New York, 1965, 98–105.

17 See A. P. Rossiter's discussion of the play in *Angel with Horns*, London, 1961, 74.

18 Rosalie Colie, *The Resources of Kind*, Berkeley, 1973.

19 See, for example, Northrop Frye, *A Natural Perspective*, New York, 1965.

20 See particularly Susan Snyder, *The Comic Matrix of Shakespeare's Tragedies*, Princeton, 1979, 91 ff.; and more generally, M. M. Bakhtin, *The Dialogic Imagination*, trans. Caryl Emerson and Michael Holquist, Austin, 1981, 84–258.

9 *Shakespeare's rhetoric of consciousness*

1 All references are to the Arden edition of *Hamlet*, ed. Harold Jenkins, London, 1982.

2 M. M. Bakhtin, *The Dialogic Imagination*, trans. Caryl Emerson and Michael Holquist, Austin, 1981, 276.

3 Harry Levin, *The Question of Hamlet*, Oxford, 1959, 157.

4 E. Cassirer, 'The influence of language on the development of

scientific thought', *Journal of Philosophy*, 39 (1942), 309–27, quoted in Jacques Derrida, 'The supplement of Copula: philosophy *before* linguistics', *Textual Strategies*, ed. Josué Harari, Ithaca, 1979, 82–120.

5   Derrida, 'Supplement of Copula', p. 91.

6   See, for example, Pierre Aubenque, 'Aristote et le langage, note annexe sur les catégories d'Aristote. A propos d'un article de M. Beneveniste', *Annales de la faculté des lettres d'Aix*, 43 (1965).

7   Derrida, 'Supplement of Copula', p. 91.

8   For an overview of theories of dramatic character, see Sanford Freedman, 'Character in a coherent fiction: on putting *King Lear* back together again', *Philosophy and Literature*, 7 (1983), 196–212.

9   Jonathan Culler, *Structuralist Poetics*, Ithaca, 1975, 29; see *inter alia*, Erving Goffman, *The Presentation of Self in Everyday Life*, Garden City, NY, 1959; Clifford Geertz, *Negara: the Theater State in Nineteenth Century Bali*, Princeton, 1980; Claude Lévi-Strauss, *Structural Anthropology*, trans. Claire Jacobson and Brodie Schoepf, Garden City, NY, 1963.

Index of plays discussed

Abusez, Les (The Deceived) 58
Adelphoe, (*The Brothers,* Terence) 49, 52, 54–5
All's Well That Ends Well (Shakespeare) 3, 59, 74, 75, 107
Aminta (Tasso) 59
Amor Costante (*Constant Love,* Piccolomini) 69
Amphitryo (Plautus) 43–5
Andria (*The Woman of Andros,* Terence) 52, 55
As You Like It (Shakespeare) 56, 60, 94–9, 100, 105

Bugbears, The (Jeffere) 58

Calandria, La (Bibbiena) 141 n. 25
Clyomon and Clamydes (anonymous) 90–3
Comedy of Errors, The (Shakespeare) 28, 59, 77–84, 94, 97, 105
Common Conditions (anonymous) 75, 90, 93
Cymbeline (Shakespeare) 97

Donna Costante, La (*The Faithful Lady,* Borghini) 69
Dutch Courtesan, The (Marston), 133 n. 9
Dyskolus (*The Grouch,* Menander) 33, 39

Epitrepontes (*The Arbitration,* Menander) 31, 35–9
Erophilomachia (*The Duel of Love and Friendship,* Oddi), 69

Fedele and Fortunio: Two Gentlemen (Munday) 58
Fedele, Il (*The Faithful One,* Pasqualigo) 58

Hamlet (Shakespeare) 122–6

Hecyra (*The Mother-in-law*, Terence) 31, 39–40, 55

Ingannati, Gl' (*The Deceived* [the Intronati], Sienese academy) 58, 60–9, 70, 76, 79, 116

Jack Juggler (anonymous) 45

Laelia (anonymous) 58
Love's Labour's Lost (Shakespeare) 3, 82, 87–90

Malcontent, The (Marston) 140 n. 3
Measure for Measure (Shakespeare) 5, 7–29, 38, 52, 59, 62, 64, 71, 80, 97, 101, 103, 108, 109–11, 119–20
Merchant of Venice, The (Shakespeare) 71
Midsummer Night's Dream, A (Shakespeare) 84–7, 90, 94, 99
Much Ado About Nothing (Shakespeare) 29, 71, 99, 107, 108, 109–20

Orestes (Euripides) 17

Pastor Fido, Il (*The Faithful Shepherd*, Guarini) 59
Pellegrina, La (*The Pilgrim*, Bargagli) 69–75
Perikeiromene (*She Who Was Shorn*, Menander) 33, 35
Pseudolus (Plautus) 46–9

Sacrifice, Le (Estienne) 58
Sacrificio, Il (*The Sacrifice*, [the Intronati), Sienese Academy) 66
Spiritata, La (*The Bugbears*, Grazzini) 58
Suppositi, I (*The Substitutes*, Ariosto) 58
Supposes (Gascoigne) 58

Tempest, The (Shakespeare) 30, 97
Twelfth Night (Shakespeare) 60–1, 99–108
Two Gentlemen of Verona, The (Shakespeare) 92

Winter's Tale, The (Shakespeare) 97

General index

Anson, John 112
Aphthonius 15–16, 37, 53; *Progymnasmata* 15
Ariosto, Ludovico 43, 57, 58, 67, 139 n. 12
Aristophanes of Byzantium 31
Aristophanes 31, 37, 39; Old Comedy 31, 39
Aristotle 14–16, 28, 31–2, 50, 51, 126–7, 137 n. 6; *Categories* 127; *Ethics* 31; *Poetics* 28–9; *Rhetoric* 14–16, 31
Ascensius, Jodocus Badius 50–1; *Praenotamenta Ascensiana* 139 n. 10
Ascham, Roger 51; *Scholemaster* 57, 145 n. 13
Auden, W. H. 7
Ausonius, 30, 137 n. 2

Bakhtin, M. M. 125, 147 n. 21
Baldwin, T. W. 30, 50, 55, 133 n. 10, 142 n. 6

Barber, C. L. 30, 143 n. 15
Barthes, Roland 2, 134 n. 1
Bargagli, Girolamo 69, 72, 75, 142 n. 27
Bargagli, Scipione 142 n. 28
Boccaccio, Giovanni 67, 92; *Decameron* 118; Gillette of Narbonne 141 n. 27
Borghini, Raffaello 69
Bradbrook, M. C. 118, 134 n. 17
Brooke, Arthur 140 n. 3

Cassirer, Ernst: language and being 126–7
Castelvetro, Lodovico: comedy and politics 67
Castiglione, Baldesar 57; *Il cortegiano* 60, 66
Cato 68
Chambers, E. W. 113
Character: defined 1–2; contemporary theories 1–2, 20; decorum 51–4; rhetoric of 5, 28, 45, 56,

74–5, 80–1, 102–3, 110–11, 114–15, 119; Renaissance sources of 14–18, 49–53; intersection with comic plot 19, 20, 28; types 31–2, 51–6, 110, 117, 139 n. 12; in Italian Renaissance comedy—development 61–6, 72–4, inner life 62–5, 74–5; in Menander—development 33–8, inner life 36–8; *novelle* 92–3

Cicero 16, 46; comedy 51; fiction and law 17–18; *De Inventione* 17; *De Natura Deorum* 16; *De Partitione Oratoria* 18; *De Senectute* 53; types 31, 52–3

Circe 57, 84

Clemen, Wolfgang: soliloquy 3–5

Coleridge, Samuel Taylor 77

Comedy: convention 20–9, 109–11, 119–20; comic types *see* character types; Italian Renaissance 56–7, 57–76, 87—*commedia grave* 69, 70, 90, compared to Shakespeare 60–5, 68, 71, 74, 75, 79, 82, 87, 90, Counter-Reformation 69, 141, disguise and mistaken identity 60–1, 72–4, emphasis on sentiment 60, 65–6, influence in England 57–8, social context 66–7; New Comedy 30–41, 43, character in 31–2, compared to Old Comedy 38–9, compared to Shakespeare 32, masks 39; Renaissance commentaries 49–54; Roman comedy—compared to Shakespeare 77–8, 84, Renaissance adaptations 45, 77–8, roleplaying 46–8, mistaken identity 44–5, 48–9

Convention: character 1–2, 20–9, 109–20; contract 21; defined 28; validity of 20

Cusanus 43

Davenant, Sir William 132 n. 2

Dialogue: linguistic features 4–5, 131 n. 13; Renaissance rhetorical exercises 15–16, 53–4; in soliloquies 4–5, 8–14, 34, 36–8, 62–5,

74–5, 80–1, 88–9, 101–3, 106–7, 114–15, 122–6

Diphilos 38

Donatus: Terence 37, 43, 49, 55, 117; comedy 50–2

Dujardin, Édouard 131 n. 13

Empson, William 12

Erasmus, Desiderius 15–16, 53; *De Conscribendis Epistolis* 15; *De Copia Rerum* 53; *De Ratione Studii* 53

Estienne, Charles 58

Euripides 16; New Comedy 31, 137 n. 3

Evanthius 50–2, 55; *De Fabula* 50

Feuillerat, Albert 140 n. 2

Florio, John 70

Garzoni, Tommaso 60–1

Gascoigne, George 58

Giraldi Cintio, Giambattista 139 n. 12

Goethe, Johann Wolfgang von 7

Gombrich, E. H. 6

Gosson, Stephen, 58, 137 n. 3

Grazzini, Anton Francesco 56

Greimas, A. J. 2

Hazlitt, William 16

Heidegger, Martin 121

Heliodorus 137 n. 3

Howard, Jean 113

Intronati, The (Sienese academy) 60, 66–7

Jeffere, John 56

Johnson, Samuel 1, 2, 103

Jonson, Ben 40

Kantorowicz, E. H. 17

Knox, Bernard 30, 137 n. 3

Lamb, Charles 105

Lenaea, The 33

Levi-Struass, Claude 2, 148 n. 9

Machiavelli, Niccolò 71
Marston, John 133 n. 9, 140 n. 3
Medici, Ferdinand de and Christine of Lorraine 70
Melanchthon, Philipp 51
Mukařovský, Jan 12, 125
Mulryne, J. R. 109

Oddi, Sforza 69, 141 n. 26
Oedipus 28
Ovid 16, 30

Pasqualigo Luigi, 58
Peacham, Henry 3
Perceforest 90
Petrarch, Francesco 57
Philemon 38
Piccolomini, Alessandro 69
Pope, Alexander 16
Propertius 30
Propp, Vladimir 2
Psychomachia 131 n. 15

Quintilian 16–17, 31–2, 52–3

Rhetores Latini Minores 17
Rhetoric: consciousness *see* character, rhetoric of; drama and 49; figures of 11, 15, 37–8, 53–4; law and 17–18; literature or fiction and 16–17; New Comedy 15, 31, 37–8, 53–4

Saintsbury, G. E. B. 15
Salingar, Leo 5, 30, 32, 59–60, 68, 141 n. 25
Saturnalia 30
Schlegel, August Wilhelm 7, 16
Shakespeare: comedies—analogues (Italian) 57–67, 70, analogues (New Comic) 30–1, analogues (Roman) 30–1, 56, 77–8, compared to early Elizabethan romantic comedy 90–3, plots criticized 1, 5, providential structure 27, 59, 74–5, substitution 27; character—development 7–14, 27–8, 79–83 (role of women in 24–8, 79–82, 95), inner life portrayed 3–5, 7–14, 59, 77–81, 85–6, 88–9, 92, 101–3, 106–7, 113–16, 122–6, judgment of 1–6, lifelikeness 1–6, 20, 28, 101–3, 109–10, 113–15; disguise 21, 24–8, 60, 95, 102–3; farce 77; losing to find 79, 105, 111; mistaken identity 2–29, 78–80, 99–102, 111–12; soliloquy *see* soliloquy and dialogue; verbal-visual 104–5; wonder 68–9, 97–9, 105
Sidonius Apollinaris 31, 39
Sidney, Sir Philip 17, 133 n. 14, 145 n. 13
Socrates 46
Soliloquy: defined 3–5; used to represent inner life in—Italian Renaissance comedy 62–5, 74–5, Menander 33–4, 36–8, Roman comedy 46–8, Shakespeare 3–5, 7–14, 28, 78–83, 88–9, 92, 101–4, 116, 122–6; *see also* dialogue

Terence, compared to Menander 39–49
Tasso, Torquato 57
Theophrastus 31, 52
Tillyard, E. M. W. 103–4, 109–10

Webster, T. B. L. 39
Weimann, Robert 30, 37–9, 143 n. 11

vraisemblance 1, 51
Vyyotsky, Lev Semenovich 131 n. 13, 141 n. 17

Willichius 53–4